*In the Hands
of the Refiner*

In the Hands of the Refiner

A Story from Lebanon

Is it not yet a very little while, and Lebanon shall be turned into a fruitful field, and the fruitful field shall be esteemed as a forest? And in that day shall the deaf hear the words of the book, and the eyes of the blind shall see out of obscurity, and out of darkness. The meek also shall increase their joy in the LORD, and the poor among men shall rejoice in the Holy One of Israel. For the terrible one is brought to naught, and the scorner is consumed, and all that watch for iniquity are cut off.
—Isaiah 29:17-20

Noor Ellias

Copyright © 2008 by Noor Ellias.

Library of Congress Control Number: 2008904966
ISBN: Hardcover   978-1-4363-4787-7
              Softcover   978-1-4363-4786-0

All rights reserved. No part of this book may be reproduced or transmitted in any form or by any means, electronic or mechanical, including photocopying, recording, or by any information storage and retrieval system, without permission in writing from the copyright owner.

Direct quotations from the Bible appear in italics.
All Bible quotations are from the King James translation unless otherwise noted.

Scripture taken from the *Holy Bible, New International Version*®. © 1973, 1978, 1984 by International Bible Society. Used by permission of International Bible society.

NIV and *New International Version* are trademarks registered in the United States Patent and Trademark office by International Bible society.

This book was printed in the United States of America.

To order additional copies of this book, contact:
Xlibris Corporation
1-888-795-4274
www.Xlibris.com
Orders@Xlibris.com
49821

Contents

Foreword by Dan Backens 7
Prologue 13

1 Hindered by Divine Intervention 19
2 Their Blood Cries Out 27
3 Walking Down Memory Lane 48
4 The Days of Wine and Roses 66
5 Miracles Never Cease 82
6 My Life in the Beqaa Valley 92
7 The Gathering Storm 103
8 The Tsunami Hits 125
9 A Bright Light in the Horizon 137
10 Shattered Dreams, Broken Lives 144
11 A Breath of Fresh Air 154
12 The Faith to Keep On 169
13 The Pressure Mounts 182
14 A Time to Reflect, a Time to Decide 197
15 A People in Revival 214
16 Victory in the Horizon 218

Epilogue 225

Foreword

Several years ago, I met Noor for the first time in church, and when I discovered she was Lebanese, I asked her how long her family had been Christians. She said, "Oh about five hundred years". I was expecting maybe one or two generations but not centuries! That would be only the first of many experiences with this dear woman that has led me to believe there is no one category for Noor. She gloriously breaks the mold of man's expectations.

Noor is first of all a passionate woman who loves her God, her family, and her heritage in a way that is fearless but also contagious. She is intelligent and strong-willed but also compassionate and witty. I have learned never to underestimate her—I have heard her pray the wallpaper right off the wall in a prayer meeting and then a moment later, be as tender as a mother with small children. In a fight, I would want her on my side; and if I was hurt, I would want her tending me.

This is a book that tells her story of walking through numbing personal pain and loss at the same time, experiencing first hand the difficult days of a war-torn Lebanon. Her rich family values give some insight to why she is a woman so well grounded even when all around her is at war.

In the Hands of the Refiner

The supernatural seems to be almost an ordinary experience for Noor. At pivotal points in her life, there always seems to be a miracle, a word from God, or an open door. When all appears to be lost, God comes through. Her story is deeply moving and tremendously exciting, and I believe it will help every reader find new hope and faith in God for their journey as well.

Pastor Dan Backens
New Life Providence

Dedication

In loving memory of my mother and father who are in a heavenly place. I say thank you with all my heart for being so faithful to God and for building in me a Christian foundation that continues to bear fruit.

And to all the Lebanese soldiers and civilians who lost life or limb throughout the years of strife that have plagued this tiny nation. May freedom and peace soon ring aloud from the steeple bells of the churches that crown the mountains of this fair land.

Acknowledgements

I would first like to acknowledge the one who inspired me to write this book and who, over the years, walked me through my personal trials and lifted me and Lebanon each time we fell—my Lord and Savior Jesus Christ and his Holy Spirit.

I also wish to thank my husband for being so patient with me as I spent long hours each day on the computer, writing my story. He took over many of the household duties so that I could spend time working on my book.

I am so grateful to my son-in-law, John, who was my right-hand man on the computer. Each time I had a technical problem, he was there to save the day.

I can never thank Pastor Farid enough for his encouragement and prayers and for allowing me to reprint his letters.

Finally, I wish to acknowledge all the courageous people of Lebanon who touched my life with their graciousness, fortitude, and zeal. To them I will always be grateful.

Prologue

Lebanon, a tiny but breathtakingly beautiful country, located on the eastern shore of the Mediterranean between Syria to the north and Israel to the south, is no stranger to wars. Throughout its long history, the people of that nation have been ravaged repeatedly by invading armies.

Their ancestors and mine, the ancient Phoenicians (the biblical Canaanites), were excellent sailors and businessmen who traveled the length of the Mediterranean in ships they constructed. They also built settlements in many of the areas where their ships landed, but never did they conquer any people group or invade any land with brute force as did the Romans, the Persians, and the Medes. Instead, they simply adapted their culture to the new environment, living peacefully among the indigenous people with whom they traded. The island of Malta is a good example of a place where the ancient Phoenicians settled.

To this very day, you can find their descendants in nearly every country of the world where they have settled in to become vibrant citizens of a new land. Most of the time, they emigrated because an invader had struck and made life unbearable for them in their homeland. At other times, they were simply adventurers seeking a new life on a distant shore. Whatever the reason for their dispersal, these resilient people left their mark on civilization by giving the world the alphabet, purple die, and so much more.

One of the greatest military strategists of all time was a Phoenician by the name of Hannibal whose ancestors settled in North Africa and built the great commercial city of Carthage. To this day, they still study his strategies at military academies around the world.

The Bible records how Solomon's Temple was built in Jerusalem by Phoenician craftsmen, whom King Hiram of Tyre sent along with the cedar wood that fortified the magnificent structure.

In addition to what the Bible says, most of what we know today about the Phoenicians comes from the historical records of their enemies. It seems odd that archaeologists have not been able to find anything scripted by the Phoenicians themselves, considering they gave the world the alphabet. Most likely, as the invading armies sacked their cities, they destroyed their libraries and writings as well.

Today, many citizens of this once thriving nation are again destitute and suffering the agony and aftermath of a new struggle. But I know that the God of history has a much better plan for this tiny nation that he mentions so many times in the Bible, and as we wait on him to fulfill Lebanon's destiny, I share my story and the story of its people during these trying times.

> *He giveth power to the faint, and to them that have no might, he increaseth strength. Even the youths shall faint and be weary, and the young men shall utterly fall: But they that wait upon the Lord shall renew their strength, they shall mount with wings as eagles, they shall run and not be weary, and they shall walk and not faint.*
>
> (Isaiah 40:29-31)

Prologue

They say that history repeats itself, and perhaps that is true in the case of Lebanon; for once again, it has become the target of invasions by armies far more powerful than its own. Through a series of events, I was personally destined to live in Lebanon through a horrendous civil war that began in the '70s and claimed the lives of thousands of its citizens.

My life, however, did not begin in Lebanon. I was born in Akron, Ohio, to parents who were immigrants from that country. My dad had come to America in 1913 to build a new life for himself, and my mother arrived in 1937 after they were married in Beirut.

As I was growing up in the '40s, life was relatively peaceful and quiet. During the years of World War II, the only disturbance we ever experienced was the sound of the sirens as they blew at night, announcing the blackout drills that were carried out by the city. I remember how everything went dark as my mother and I sat on the steps that led to our first-floor apartment, waiting for the electricity to come back. Akron at that time was the rubber capital of the world, and I was constantly reminded of that fact by the bruising scent that emanated from the smokestacks of the BF Goodrich tire and rubber company located only three blocks away from our house.

Akron was home to a typical and rather large Middle Eastern community, which was represented by three churches: Greek Orthodox, Maronite Catholic, and Melkite Catholic. Like all ethnic groups, the Lebanese loved mingling with each other; however, they never lived in ghettos. This made it easy for them to adapt to their new environment and build friendships outside their own community. But never did they leave their favorite Lebanese foods and traditions. Each church had its yearly picnic when all other churches and friends were invited to attend. Lebanese food, folkloric dance, and music were the order of the day; and it was wonderful.

That first generation of immigrants was the glue that kept the unity among the Lebanese, with all of the beautiful traditions, alive in the hearts of their children and grandchildren.

I'll never forget one summer day when, as a child of nine, something awesome happened to me. My parents, along with two other families, decided to go on a Sunday picnic after church at one of the municipal parks. Later on that evening, as the sun gently dipped below the horizon, the intense blue color of the northern sky suddenly captured my attention. I left the group and walked by myself toward a lovely green meadow a good distance away from our table. With my hands behind my head, I laid back on the grass and gazed at the stars that were shining like a million crystal chandeliers; an unusual sight for our city. I believe God gave me what I would later describe as a "Davidic moment." Certainly many of his psalms were inspired by the wonders of that very same sky he also observed over three thousand years ago. As I stared in amazement, I felt the indescribable majesty and grandeur of a creator God rise up in me. I could no longer grasp the enormity of the universe and its maker compared to my own size. It was like comparing one grain of sand to all the oceans of the world. I began to shake uncontrollably as he revealed his wonder and glory to a nine-year-old girl. I remember so clearly what I said to him. "Oh God, how big you are and how small I am." I know he wanted to tell me something that day even though I did not fully comprehend what it was then. I believe this was the evidence of one of the Psalms of David that I did not read until years later.

O Lord our Lord, how excellent is Thy name in all the earth! who hast set thy glory above the heavens. Out of the mouth of babes and sucklings hast Thou ordained strength . . . When I consider

Thy heavens, the work of thy fingers, the moon and the stars, which Thou hast ordained; What is man, that thou art mindful of him? and the son of man, that Thou visitest him. For Thou hast made him a little lower than the angels, and hast crowned him with glory and honor. Thou madest him to have dominion over the works of Thy hands; Thou hast put all things under his feet.

(Psalm 8:1-3)

I had also gone through grade school when teachers were able to punish students, if necessary, without fear of being slapped with a lawsuit by some irked parent or, at the very least, reprimanded by the principal. Each morning, we gladly recited the Lord's Prayer in our classroom and the Pledge of Allegiance as we stood proudly before the American flag.

Our parents and mentors had successfully instilled in us a deep respect for authority, and it paid off. Student violence was practically nonexistent. To top it off, I had a typical Middle Eastern mama who was very protective. I never had to carry a house key because when I came home from school, she was always there at the door to greet me. I can never forget how she would place me on full alert every morning as I prepared to leave for school. Before she gave me a big hug and sent me on my way, she would say in a loving yet firm voice, "Don't you ever talk to strangers or believe anyone who might try to tell you that I sent them to bring you home. Understood?"

I definitely understood at a very early age that there were some bad guys on the streets, and that I was to set my face like a flint and not blink an eye or talk to any stranger passing by, and it worked. However, this peaceful lifestyle was a sharp contrast to what I would be experiencing at a future-appointed time.

By the age of eleven, I learned about a promise Dad had made to his in-laws before his wedding that he would one day return with his wife to live permanently in Lebanon. After I was born, I automatically became a part of that promise. There certainly were times I felt that I was being uprooted although mother had very wisely taken me at the age of twelve for an extended trip to Lebanon where I became acquainted with a new culture. Several months after I graduated from the University of Akron in 1960, Dad retired and fulfilled his promise to return to his homeland in 1961—thus my life was changed forever.

In 1963, I fell in love and married Roy, a handsome young Lebanese Air Force officer. Little did I know I would soon be experiencing a personal struggle that would bring me to my knees, and several years later, be enduring the hardships of a long and tumultuous civil war.

By then, I had every reason to justify taking my family and leaving, but a deep love for Lebanon and its people that never diminished in spite of the chaos kept me there. I refused to entertain the thought of forsaking my home permanently. Under pressure, we soon discover that the greatest element in our survival kit is the gift of hope that keeps us going. It was a long wait, and finally in 1990, peace did return to the land.

By 1997, however, we were semiretired and living with our two daughters in America while they were finishing their graduate studies in Virginia. Nevertheless, my husband and I went back to our home in Beirut every summer and spent at least three months there. Only this time, the summer of 2006 was quite different, and I knew it was time to tell my story. However I did change the names of some of the people to protect their privacy.

Chapter 1

Hindered by Divine Intervention

The steps of a good man are ordered by the Lord: and he delighteth in his way. Though he fall, he shall not be utterly cast down: for the Lord upholdeth him with his hand.
—*Psalm 37:23, 24*

On Saturday July 8, Roy, his sister Fadwa, and I would have arrived in Beirut five days before the devastating Israeli air strikes on Southern Lebanon and Beirut began. However, something happened that hindered us from completing our trip. No sooner had we boarded the plane on the second part of our journey than Roy's blood pressure flared up. As paramedics checked him out, it became apparent that it was wiser to delay our departure date. Thus Fadwa and I gathered our belongings and got off the plane.

Concern soon turned to frustration and disappointment as we discovered that all flights into Lebanon for that month were completely booked. Almost one hour and many attempts later, a valiant ticketing agent was able to reroute our itinerary and find us the only space available on a flight leaving for Beirut two weeks later.

It was nearing midnight, and as there were no flights that could get us back home that evening, the ground attendant accompanied us to where we took a shuttle to the motel. By then, we were utterly exhausted.

The next afternoon, Roy's blood pressure had gone back to normal, and we returned to the airport, collected our luggage, and got on the only plane scheduled that day for Norfolk International Airport. A week later, our flight plans were interrupted once again, not by an unexpected health crisis, but by the thirty-three days of ceaseless Israeli ground and air assaults. This was when I knew in my spirit it had to be divine intervention that prevented us from completing our trip.

My sister-in-law, Fadwa, had been visiting us from Lebanon. Although in excellent health, she was nearly eighty years old and had never been out of her own country except for a few short visits to an Orthodox convent in Syria and a tour of Damascus. My daughter made Fadwa's first real trip abroad possible as she would never have dreamed of traveling to a distant land so late in life. It was, therefore, no surprise that she considered her trip to America such a wonderful and unforgettable experience. However, her joy soon turned to sorrow as she watched on the news her country being ravaged. We could only pray for God to manifest his mercy over Lebanon and wait on that nation to again open its doors for us to return. It took two long and painful months before we were able to set foot in Lebanon.

After a ceasefire finally went into effect, I called the airlines and rebooked for September 12. We hoped that by then, the Beirut airport runways would be repaired; and our plane would not be forced to land in Amman, Jordan, to be searched by Israeli Special Forces. We began to pray fervently, and in less than a week, God answered our prayers. A Qatar Airways passenger plane coming into Beirut challenged the Israeli blockade by refusing to land in Jordan, and to everyone's relief, the Israelis did not take it down as they had formerly threatened to do. This courageous but daring act by the pilot opened the door for other planes to land directly at Beirut International Airport.

It was during this long wait that God gave me the desire and inspiration to write this book. For the fire of the Holy Spirit had fused my soul even more deeply to that of Lebanon's, compelling me to tell our story.

With our travel plans on hold, I began to witness once again the tragedy of human suffering and degradation on a much larger scale than ever before. I was helplessly watching—unable to do anything—unable to make a difference. The images on TV appeared like a replay of the devastated war zones of World War II, not on a continent, but in a tiny country no bigger than the size of Connecticut.

This new conflict brought back memories that took me in time to the fifteen years of a senseless struggle that began in 1975. It also included both a Syrian and Israeli occupation as well as two major Israeli invasions. But for the grace of God, we too could have become nameless casualties forgotten by the tides of time. However, we survived. Thus forever etched in my memory would be the events of those dark brutal years.

I cannot forget how the international media seemed indifferent to the plight of Lebanon's people. Even now, my heart is wounded afresh when I remember the thousands of Lebanese who were kidnapped or killed by terrorists and invading armies in the chaos of the civil war. Only the handful of internationals who were victims of similar kidnappings were found worthy of mention by the international news media while the Lebanese who had suffered the same fate were ignored. And those who survived would themselves be depicted as terrorists, profiled and sometimes grossly mistreated at airports when their only sin was attempting to seek temporary refuge in some country outside their own. Those who could not afford to leave were forced to tolerate life under the impossible conditions the war imposed on them. We were among those who remained in Beirut except for a period of nine months when we left for America in the spring of '76.

Roy was on active duty in the Lebanese Air Force. Being on full alert, he rarely ever came home. I did not intend to leave him behind in the midst of battle for the safety of American soil. My destiny was linked to that part of the world, and I was not about to turn my back on all that had meant so much to me. I also knew in my heart that God had other plans for my life, and that He would protect my family through it all. Prayer now became as natural as breathing, and it miraculously sustained me during that long season of tribulation.

For those who have never seen the beauty of Beirut, it was and still is the envy of its Middle Eastern neighbors. This city of magnificent nineteenth—and early-twentieth-century French and modern architecture, artistically landscaped gardens, beautiful sidewalk cafes, and plush hotels had been rebuilt after the civil war ended beginning in 1990. Under the direction of former Prime Minister Rafic Hariri, downtown Beirut was once again bustling with activity; a modern city filled with restaurants, cafes, and boutiques; a historic city filled with ruins dating back to the Roman period, the Hellenistic period, even as far back as the Iron and Bronze age. Just a few steps away

Hindered by Divine Intervention

in an area directly parallel to these streets is the archaeological site of the ancient Berytus (Beirut) School of Law built by the Romans in the middle of the third century AD. The destruction caused by the civil war gave archaeologists the opportunity to dig under the rubble, revealing newer and larger sites. To the surprise of many, it contained more than four thousand years of human history dating back to the Phoenicians.

Now that peace had returned, you could bump shoulders with hundreds of people taking brisk evening walks without fear of having some criminal element attack you on the street. Roy and I were among those who enjoyed walking in the cool of the night along the boulevard called the Corniche, which surrounds the western tip of Beirut that juts into the Mediterranean. That whole area would cast the glitter of its bright city lights into the dark blue waters of the sea like thousands of brilliant diamonds.

During the clear summer evenings, we would often stop and watch the beauty of a Lebanese sunset. As it made its descent into the sparkling Mediterranean, the sky would burst with the wild fiery colors of orange and yellow set against a canopy of blue.

We also passed the numerous restaurants and street cafes that lined the boulevard on both sides. Sometimes during our morning walks, we would stop at one of the many pastry shops, both Lebanese and European, and eat a delicious breakfast of a sweet called *knaffi* with cheese. It was served warm and dripping with a delectable syrup that contained lemon blossom and rose essence. The Lebanese were always famous for having the richest and tastiest cuisine in the Middle East, and in the realm of pastries and sweets, they excelled.

Sadly, the people had only a few short years to catch their breath. Suddenly, like a powerful burst of lightning, a new and more deadly encounter would begin. Now Beirut Central District, as well as many other areas, became a ghost town—no more laughter, no more pithy conversations, no more anything. The cruelest bombings this country had ever experienced were ravaging "the Pearl of the Middle East" as well as the South.

It reminded me of a poem written by Khalil Gibran, (1883-1931) Lebanon's brilliant artist and poet, in memory of the thousands of Lebanese who died during the imposed famine of 1916. It was in his adopted country, America, where he poured out his heart, lamenting his countrymen and homeland. This poem is as relevant today as it was nearly a century ago. A portion of it reads:

> *The knolls of my country are submerged*
> *By tears and blood, for my people and*
> *My beloved are gone, and I am here*
> *Living as I did when my people and my*
> *Beloved were enjoying life and the*
> *Bounty of life, and when the hills of*
> *My country were blessed and engulfed*
> *By the light of the sun.*
> *They died because the vipers and*
> *Sons of vipers spat out poison into*
> *The space where the Holy Cedars and*
> *The roses and the jasmine breathe* [1]

Back then, the people were still living under the tyranny of the Turkish Ottoman Empire that controlled all of the Middle East for more than four hundred years.

---

[1] "Dead Are My People" from *The Treasured Writings of Khalil Gibran,* (Castle Books, 1981)

During World War I, the Lebanese, whose land flowed with milk and honey, were dying from a manmade famine. The Entente Powers had laid siege to the region, which included Lebanon, in order to weaken their enemy, the Ottomans. Of course, the Turkish soldiers had no intention of ever going hungry, so they confiscated all the grain and vegetables the farmers had raised or stored, not only to feed themselves, but their horses as well; and alas, no food for the masses. You could pass by any road and see the emaciated faces of little children and the bodies of victims who died of hunger.

As a young boy, my father was an eyewitness to the humiliation the people of Lebanon suffered at the hands of the oppressor. In one of our conversations, he told me how the Ottoman Turks desecrated village churches by turning them into stables for their horses. Luckily, Dad's home village, Niha, was built on one of the higher mountains in the Chouf area 3,500 feet above sea level. The dangerously winding road that led to the edge of the village had nine twists and turns on one side of the mountain, making it barely accessible, especially during the winter months. Thus Niha was spared a constant Turkish presence and the loss of its food supply. The lower regions were not so lucky. However, before the siege ever began, God, in his infinite mercy, opened the door for Dad to immigrate to America.

One particular victim of Ottoman tyranny was my mother's uncle, a prominent young physician in his late thirties. Turkish soldiers had stopped his carriage one day when he was on a medical call and forcibly dragged him out. They asked him questions, called him a Christian dog and began beating him savagely on his back. Afterward, they threw him into his carriage and sent him home. The next night, his kidneys began to shut down, and he died in the arms of his wife, Emily, shortly after. As she recounted the story to me, she clearly remembered her husband's last words to her. "There are no medicines that can help me now. I'm dying. Just take care of our little boys."

Even if science had discovered a drug that might have saved the young doctor's life, no medical remedy has yet to be found for the worst plague of all—the universal human condition of a depraved heart. This ailment that God calls sin has the ability to kill, not only the body, but the soul as well. There has never been, or ever will be, a scientific, political, or sociological antidote for this kind of heart problem. Its remedy lies in the hands of a holy and loving God, who one day promises healing for this earth and for all who believe in his Word. Until then, we will continue to see wars and human suffering perpetrated at the hands of evil men.

Yet as Lebanon's story and mine unfold, I want you to experience with me those thrilling moments of victory that are birthed in the midst of tragedy; and through it all, to discover the power of a surrendered life to God's will and purpose.

Chapter 2

Their Blood Cries Out

And the LORD said unto Cain: Where is Abel thy Brother. And he said, I know not: Am I my brothers keeper?
—**Genesis 4:9**

It was Sunday, July 16, 2006. Eva and her beautiful two-year-old daughter arrived at the home of Pastor Farid in a village that overlooks the eastern sector of Beirut and the blue Mediterranean—now blurred by clouds of dusty gray smoke from the explosion of bombs and missiles. Eva's sister and brother-in-law had accompanied her through the harrowing experience of constant air strikes and whatever dangers that lay on the road between the city of Tyre in the south and Beirut.

Unfortunately, Eva's husband was caught somewhere in the cross fire and could not make the rendezvous with his wife to escape the carnage that Israeli bombing would produce. However, she and her family were welcomed and made to feel at home in the place that would be for some time their shelter; for they all had become refugees.

Later on that day, she was able to contact her husband who still had his cell phone with him. He was so grateful that his wife and daughter had made it to safety when others, who also were trying to escape, did not. That same evening, however, Pastor Farid turned the TV on to hear the latest news and watch a live broadcast, showing the results of Israeli shelling in the city of Tyre. As the camera panned in on the bodies of those who were in a civilian building they had targeted, Eva recognized two lifeless forms on the ground in a pool of blood—her husband and his brother. That was the last time she ever saw her husband again. Crumpling as she fell to the floor from the shock, there would be no consoling her. There would be no consoling many who, like her, had lost loved ones in this so-called war on terrorism. Only the militiamen who were supposed to be the target were not dying. Instead, those slain were mostly innocent men, women, and children along with the elderly. One week later, as Sunday rolled around, the Israelis had already made four thousand air strikes over Lebanon according to news reports.

Life now became unbearable with the ceaseless shelling, both day and night, of civilian buildings or people who were unlucky enough to be in vehicles on some highway, making a run for their lives. I watched CNN and the news coverage about the infrastructure of Lebanon being destroyed with precision. Many utility plants, such as those supplying electricity, were also targeted. The Beirut Airport runways were bombed several times, and the roads and bridges that carried people to safety received their share of air strikes. Complete quarters in southern Beirut were razed, and suddenly a big part of this beautiful city resembled London after the blitz. The country that people called the Switzerland of the Middle East became the epitome of Dante's "Inferno."

To the Lebanese people and the Lebanese government, both innocent of the ploys of Hizballah, it appeared as if Israel was more bent on the annihilation of a sovereign state rather than the destruction of the insurgency that had angered them by kidnapping two of their soldiers as leverage for a trade-off of prisoners.

Thousands of Americans and other foreigners on vacation in Lebanon had to be evacuated. As the U.S. State Department began deploying their ships and helicopters for the task, it appeared evident to me that America was guaranteed safety in the harbors where the evacuation would take place. It was my understanding that the U.S. government normally maintained no contact whatsoever with Hizballah, so I thought it was strange that this militia never fired a single missile in order to wreak havoc on the evacuation process. Perhaps there was some redeeming quality we had missed.

Just six years prior in May of 2000, after more than twenty years of Israeli occupation, Hizballah fighters succeeded in forcing an Israeli withdrawal from Lebanese territory (with the exception of the Shebaa Farms). Since then, Hizballah has continued to maintain an armed presence that few Lebanese wanted, especially the Christians and Sunni Muslims. Every other militia that fought in the civil war had been dismantled while Hizballah continued to operate in Southern Lebanon as a resistance movement.

At the beginning of the civil war in 1975, the military establishment of Lebanon was intentionally stripped of its power by Lebanese proxy politicians while at the same time more militias of every shape and color started to emerge. In reality, the leaders of these militias were no more than tribal warlords dressed in fancy suits and perhaps, carrying a degree from some university. To make matters worse, mercenaries entered illegally through the borders of Syria from Iran, Libya, Iraq, and Jordan to join the Islamic militias that had formed. Even Israel collaborated with one of the Christian militias, making certain every ruthless neighbor in the region was represented in this senseless war.

During that same period, France would no longer sell any spare parts for the Mirage jet fighters the Lebanese Air Force had purchased for the defense of their country. They were the same planes that Roy received his technical training on during his stay in France in 1967. In fact, the whole of the Western world, including America, refused to sell this tiny nation any arms to defend itself. To this very day, the Lebanese Armed Forces have not fully recovered. With this strange background in mind, I saw Israel, in 2006, demanding that the Lebanese government, on its own, deploy their military to the South and forcibly dismantle Hizballah. With merely an armory of old conventional weapons and an air force that still did not have a single plane or defense missile, it would not take a rocket scientist to figure out the feasibility of such a task. Besides, Hizballah was considered a Lebanese resistance movement rather than a terrorist group, as the West had labeled it.

The civil war forced my family and me to live under similar dismal conditions. I knew quite well what the people were going through again. I remember getting used to having only three or four hours of electricity per day, and sometimes none at all, as well as carrying gallons of drinking water up to our sixth-floor apartment. After all, no electricity meant no elevator. I quickly learned by experience the meaning of water conservation.

In those days, my first task was to fill the bathtub and some kitchen utensils to the brim before the municipality cut off the electricity and water supply. In that manner, we insured ourselves enough water for at least ten days or more, if necessary. Standing in a small basin, we each bathed in less than a gallon of water that

I heated on the stove. We then used what we saved for some other purpose. I counted the precious drops and conserved them for "the royal flush." I know that only a living God could have given us the stamina and patience to endure fifteen years of hardship under these conditions.

Although food was available throughout the civil war, the valiant citizens of Beirut still had to worry about falling prey to a sniper's bullet while standing in an extremely long breadline at some bakery or behind a hundred other cars waiting to purchase a few gallons of rationed gasoline.

In this new war on terrorism, Israel imposed a blockade, which meant no food or medical supplies coming into the country. At the same time, Israeli bombs targeted food depots and delivery trucks under the pretext that they were hiding weapons while the multiple thousands of cluster bombs they dropped over Southern Lebanon lay silently on the ground, or in a tree, until some innocent passerby touched one. After the ceasefire, many Lebanese civilians did just that as they went to check their orchards and paid the ultimate price with their lives. Some hospitals also got in the way, including a Red Cross ambulance that was trying to help the injured.

The Israelis even managed to cause a major environmental disaster by illegally targeting the storage tanks of a power plant located thirty miles south of Beirut, thus dumping into the Mediterranean an estimated fifteen to twenty thousand tons of fuel oil. It damaged the coastal waters from Sidon all the way to Tripoli in the north, devastating the entire coastline of Lebanon, killing fish and birds as well as destroying the seabed where fish spawn. No one, not even the foreign experts who later participated in the cleaning process, ever believed that this barbaric act was unintentional. The Israelis know quite well that the water currents travel north and never south; thus, none of the spill would ever affect their coastline. Sadly, Palm Island, a wildlife reserve five miles off the coast of Tripoli and home to many endangered species, was devastated with pitch contamination. Yet I did not hear any member of the world community speak out publicly against this act as they had done when Saddam Hussein polluted the waters of Kuwait with oil spills. It seemed that no civilian sector, commercial or otherwise, was spared this round of events.

The Lebanese are, by nature, lovers of freedom and never got used to having their land occupied by some invading army, so they always looked for opportunities to demonstrate against each occupation. Sometimes, two occupiers lived simultaneously on the same piece of land called Lebanon, just as Syria and Israel did for more than twenty years. In my opinion, they certainly were strange bedfellows. When they got angry at each other, they killed the Lebanese.

Then there were the Palestinians who played a major role in the civil war back in the '70s. To this very day, they still live in camps in Northern and Southern Lebanon, as well as in parts of Beirut. Sadly, the Palestinian issue is still a festering wound that never seems to heal while it continues to adversely affect Lebanon's well being.

As recently as 2005, the one responsible for the reconstruction of Lebanon, former Prime Minister Rafic Hariri, was assassinated. My husband and I drove to the very spot where the bomb that killed him and his companions, along with a fellow member of parliament, exploded. The area was still cordoned off, but as I looked, it appeared as if a bunker buster had hit the area. It seemed obvious to me that the bomb was planted underground. That particular street was under construction for many months, and certainly, placing a bomb deep into the soil before the road was ever paved would have been easy. It was only a matter of timing when the explosion would take place.

This was followed by the murder of Gebran Tueni, former editor and publisher of one of the most prestigious Arabic newspapers in the Middle East, *An-Nahar*. He had committed the unpardonable sin of being an outspoken critic of the Syrian presence in Lebanon. Unfortunately, after returning from his self-imposed exile in France, Gebran received a loyal citizen's welcome—a bomb detonated in a car that was parked at one of the spots he drove by daily on his way home.

I met Mr. Tueni in the summer of 2000 during an interview he gave for a TV special that was set up for the jubilee year, celebrating the birth of Christ. When I heard the news of his death, I could not help but grieve even though I had met him only once. This courageous young man had made a deep impression on all who were present that day for the taping of the interview.

Even during the civil war, I saw Lebanon experience one political assassination after another as well as kidnappings by the militias and occupiers who apparently tolerated neither disobedience nor criticism. Thus thousands of Lebanese found themselves in either Syrian or Israeli prisons. To date, there are still many Lebanese unaccounted for who were kidnapped by the occupying forces. This situation has left their families without any closure, not knowing whether they are alive or dead. Although the Syrians continue to deny there are any Lebanese citizens left in their infamous jails, the families of the kidnapped say otherwise.

Miraculously, whenever there was an interim of peace and quiet, Lebanon would swiftly recover while its people bounced back doing what Lebanese do best—working, studying, enjoying life, and being hospitable to friends and outsiders alike. You never felt like a stranger in Lebanon.

One of the best examples of this spirit of hospitality and goodness were my own parents. You did not need to phone them to schedule a visit. You could come any time, and they would stop whatever it was they were doing to welcome you and make you feel at home. If you happened to arrive before lunch, they would invite you to eat with them and would rarely take no for an answer. Being an awesome cook, Mom would make a meal fit for a king whenever they entertained guests for dinner. However, before the clouds of civil strife had gathered, my parents were spared the terrible pain of seeing their beautiful country raped and ravaged by an inhumane war. By 1969, they both had gone to be with the Lord, and I would live to experience the suffering of a people caught in the cross fire and to tell their story and mine.

In the summer of 2005, my husband and I flew into Beirut as usual, rejoicing that the Syrians had finally withdrawn their military presence from Lebanese soil. We returned to the States in September with a renewed hope for the continuation of peace and stability as things appeared to be going back to normal. Then in July, the kidnapping of two Israeli soldiers by Hizballah occurred. Immediately the bombing began; and the carnage, never before experienced on such a scale in Lebanon, appeared to dash all hope of recovery in the hearts of so many of Lebanon's people.

This time, I feared there would be more than just the death of civilians, the demolition of buildings, and the destruction of farmland in the aftermath. For the hideous smell of the smoke and dust from debris that polluted the air would surely take its toll on the lives of those who inhaled its toxic fumes long after the bombings ceased. Who would ever know what pollutants the missiles had activated. Pastor Farid told me that no one had ever smelled this kind of pungent odor before, not even when the Israelis bombed Beirut in 1983. I was there then, and know from experience that no such fumes were present in the air during that particular invasion.

What made matters worse is the fact that Lebanon has a land mass of only 4,035 square miles, making it difficult for innocent civilians to hide from the bombing and the aftermath. The nine hundred thousand displaced souls could only go to where their gracious and hospitable countrymen would open their hearts, homes, and churches to shelter them. However, the possibility of these shelters also becoming targets of the systematic and precise Israeli shelling was strong. It already was apparent that Hizballah strongholds were not the only targets our southern neighbor was bombing.

On July 24, I received the following e-mail from Pastor Farid in Lebanon, and with his permission, I have printed it. You can sense how distraught he was just by the rough English grammar he used. Perhaps now my readers can better understand the feelings and emotions of one who is experiencing the shock and pain of events out of his control as he speaks out in his own words. In his letters, he always calls me and my husband *Mom* and *Dad*, and we always think of him as our spiritual son in the Lord:

Hi Mom,

Praise the Lord I am still able to communicate,

. . . .—You will find Hiroshima in some areas!

The Israelis are only killing civilians, only by yesterday they have killed 3 Hizballah resistant's (militants)—

So after killing 360 Civilians and mostly children and babes they kill 3 Hizballah—(Formula:360 to 3 which means 120civilians to 1 Hiz.soldier)

If you count it, well, using this formula that the USA supports, how many civilians have to be killed to finish off the 300.000 Hizballah resistant's.(militants) You will have to add two Zeros—Which means 36 000 000 (This is 36 million) we are 3 Million in Lebanon, so they will finish all the civilians in Lebanon before killing 3000—

I am not counting the other part!

This is what they are talking about right now! This has to stop right NOW!

They ask people to evacuate, while evacuating, they attack them on the roads, cars, buses, even Motorbikes, tens of them! Hundreds are dying on the roads, believe it or not.

You know Lee the Canadian gentleman and his family, wife and children. He is a member of my church and stuck in a village in South Lebanon) he is afraid to leave there and come here because he knows and sees how they are hitting civilians on the roads—He told me I prefer dying in my house rather than the roads. He said, now is the time when God wants to use me to feel, help and pray!

No communication between Beirut and the North—it is not easy to get a line to talk to the rest of the country.

I have three teams in my Church now are planning with me and Gaby to do special children programs, praise the Lord.... We are taking charge of three schools around us filled with refugees.

Since there are organizations taking some care of food, we have decided to care for women, babies and children—we bought a stock of underwear for women (top and sleeps) and sleeps, towels, soap, tooth brushes.... milk and other health sweets for children—We gathered two cars full of summer clothes and shoes up to now and distributing it—

Our program in each school is up to 2 hours with Children—some talk with adults and women.

We are doing games, education on health and many things and Bible stories, Christian songs and prayers.

We were 15 persons in the mission center this morning planning, organizing the boxes, etc....

Gaby and Sara are buying stocks for distribution.

Yes, you might think we are risking our lives, yes this is somehow true! My house is full of people as well as the apartment in our building in the mountain—The Baptist seminary is full—People keep coming in large numbers—Official schools are packed—The small houses (one bed room) have 3 families each—(You know the Muslim families, the small family is 8)—I personally don't expect the refugees will go home before few months of ceasing fire.

> I think the government will face a lot of pressure from those who lost their relatives, their companies, their houses, their factories, 3 billion dollars up to this hour! Add this to our 44 Billion dollar debt!
>
> Now, Condolissa Rice is meeting with our P. M. Seniora, God have mercy!
>
> Only a miracle can save us! That's why we are still in Lebanon, we want to see miracles.
>
> Now you have some hints of what to pray for,
>
> Be Blessed,
>
> Keep writing, this will keep me encouraged!
>
> Farid

Pastor Farid was lucky to have had times of electricity so that he could send an e-mail. Initially it was extremely difficult to even get a call through as people relied more on cell phones until the Israelis struck the cell tower. It would be the brave Lebanese soldiers who constantly placed their lives in harm's way, climbing the utility poles and repairing the damage to either phone or electrical lines.

The next day, as I opened my computer to read the news coming out of Lebanon, one very descriptive and heart-wrenching article caught my attention. A foreign newspaper correspondent living in Beirut wrote it. He had been there for many years, and it appeared that he was still there in spite of the shelling. His article told the story of how he had accompanied four Lebanese soldiers who were on their way to repair electrical power lines that the Israelis had just hit. They were very caring about his safety, and after they had completed the task, they quickly took him back to the hotel as there was still the danger of another immediate air strike in the vicinity. They wasted no time in returning to their own barracks. That night, as the soldiers were preparing to retire, the Israelis targeted the barracks where they slept; and all four men were killed. The following day, this columnist learned about the tragedy, and you could sense from his article the pain he was experiencing as he wrote. These were not insurgents hiding in some civilian building. They were members of Lebanon's regular army, and Israel would have to create another flimsy excuse for this so-called blunder.

Such stories of bravery, however, were not new to me since I was a military wife who had repeatedly witnessed the courage of the men in uniform. Throughout the civil war they would go to repair power lines and restore electricity or rebuild bridges as the civilians responsible could not even get to work, let alone do the job.

Pastor Farid later sent me another e-mail describing the courage of a group of inhabitants from the Beqaa Valley who escaped the air attacks over their homes. They found refuge in the churches of Beirut and its suburbs. Farid had received one such group of about fifty brave souls who took the risk of being killed from the air while making a run for their lives.

Before the attack, the Israelis had dropped flyers over their homes, warning them to clear out because the bomb runs would soon begin. The problem was that Israel had given warnings of this nature before in Southern Lebanon but then bombed the very people they were telling to clear out. There was no guarantee their fate would not be the same. This was a grueling two-hour trip by car—if all went well. Thankfully, they did make it safely, and Farid welcomed them by locating homes among the people of his congregation and other buildings where they could stay for as long as they needed.

July 27 came, and the media coverage on television continued to show the carnage, which had now expanded from one end of the country to the other. In just twelve days, the number of Lebanese casualties grew to over six hundred. As the air strikes widened, many more civilians were dying rather than Hizballah fighters. My heart sank at the horror that was being played out on TV before my very eyes, and I needed to make sense of it all. I cried out and asked God to please show me why this was all happening, and then the next day, Pastor Farid sent me another e-mail. It did not answer my question of why, but it surely revealed to me how God operates in times of adversity:

> Last Sunday a family of 5 Muslim people visited us at the Church Sunday service, they gave their lives to the Lord and shared with us communion. Wednesday, a few other families wanted to come, however, I did not think it would have been appropriate because I was teaching on how to win non-Christians to the Lord. (Yes, that would have been odd)
>
> I promised them for Sunday! This is the good part . . . . Farid.

Learning that precious souls were finding consolation in a Savior forever ready to welcome his children into the kingdom of God was the news I needed to hear. In all of their sufferings, God was still there, saving their souls and healing their wounded hearts.

Of course, other e-mails from Pastor Farid followed, detailing more of the horrific tales he heard from refugees who survived the Israeli assault on their villages in Southern Lebanon. What they saw of death and destruction while making the perilous journey on roads that barely existed is too graphic to describe, for most of the charred and dismembered bodies they saw were those of little children.

Lee, the Canadian gentleman, whom Pastor Farid had mentioned in his e-mail, lived permanently in the south and decided not to leave. Since he and his wife had already planned before the attack to send their daughter to Canada to study, they made their way to the port of Tyre. There, he bid an emotional farewell to his wife and teenage daughter while he and his younger children stayed behind. Lee admitted he didn't want to leave Lebanon during the crisis. It was also his wife's intention to rejoin him a few days later.

I was deeply moved and blessed to know that there were people like him who had the courage to remain under God's calling. As I read his letter, it brought to mind the sermon my own pastor had preached at our church in Virginia only a week before. In his message he said, "The safest place on earth to be is in the will of God." Lee would have applauded those words since he was a living testament to the truth of that statement. I received permission to reprint the e-mail he sent in response to those who criticized his decision to remain with his other children:

> Hi,
>
> In my previous letter about sending my wife and daughter off on a luxury liner—albeit only for a short cruise to Cyprus, I said I would answer the question as to, why split the family up and why stay? Given all the risk and uncertainty, given the seemingly increasing tempo of bombing and threats, why stay?
>
> First of all, life for us-my wife and I—is more than an issue of safety and security. It is more than an issue of what is best for us financially and personally. Our faith, and the direction we believe we have from God, leads us to many times put aside our issues of safety, security, and personal

well being in order to follow through on what He asks us to do. Now I realize that this is the decision my wife & I have made—and that we cannot assume our children are at the same place as we, nor should we force such decisions on them when they really do not understand them. In addition I agree completely that we should not place our children needlessly at risk. But by leaving here, what "risk" do we incur by choosing to live in the West? There's hardly a family we know that does not have one or more children damaged/traumatized either by the social ostracism of the schools, by family abuse, by drugs or by the random violence of North American society. Little of that is found here. It is far easier to hide from bombs than from the porn, the violence, the rants, the drugs and other addictions of N. American society—IF you believe that hiding is the way to handle it! But there is something far more insidious than any of those "risks" mentioned above, and I will come to it in a moment.

 I personally do not believe that hiding is an effective way of handling either the physical bombs (our current situation) or the social bombs (the western cultural situation). Likewise, it is easier to pour concrete and repair a bridge than to try to unravel the evil of such societal abuse and violence. Children here can be shielded from much of the violence of war—should the parents choose to do so—and there is hardly a parent here, from the poorest to the richest, that will not do everything in their power to do just that

 Perhaps one of the most heart chilling scenes I have ever seen was a picture in a local Lebanese paper a couple days ago. No, it was not the charred and broken bodies of children or families. It was a picture of two healthy young Isr'li girls, aged about 9 and 11. Behind them in the background you see the tanks that are shelling the south of Lebanon and around them stacks of 120mm shells. The spine-chilling picture shows them cheerfully scrawling chalk messages on the tips of those shells. You can be sure they were not love letters.

The young guys in the computer store that showed me the picture were incensed and angrily demanded "How can there ever be peace when they are doing that?" "Isn't the only hope there the new generation? (assumed to be free of the legacy of hurt and war). He swore and turned away in disgust. And their thought is—this is the West. This is the fruit of a world where the powerful West tries to make the whole world live one way and think one way. Where those that disagree—for any reason at all, are labelled as "terrorists" and can then be detained for years without charges, subjected to all kinds of the latest psychological torture designed to destroy their ability to even think, tried in closed courts on evidence they never see—but what is worst of all—these people are seen as deviants, they are seen as somehow subhuman and deserving of such a fate. Is this the world I want to take my children to?

The West lives in fear. There is an almost palpable feeling of fear and victimization in the media and lives of those in N. America. It is this fear that powers the American drive to remake the world in its own image—for the people who are part of the system will never rise up against it. They simply have too much to lose. People here fear Isr'li bombs, not their culture and certainly not their values. That largely western culture and values are seen by most to be insidious and evil even though they love the toys. Yet the West, at heart, fears Arab values and culture (not its bombs and certainly not its toys), for it has an innate morality, humanity, and communal wholeness long ago abandoned in the West. So when it comes to risk, there are many things to weigh when we think of our children and what world we will expose them to.

But having said all of that, there really is one main reason we are here. Because Paul's presence on the boat, (Acts 27:24) God saved those that were with him. Lots' presence in Sodom delayed its destruction to the last possible minute.

The gospel never was a set of rules. It is more than a message of love. It is the presence of the Spirit of God living in us. That Spirit gives us a message, and enables us to love & forgive. That Spirit's presence in us also brings protection to those around us when we choose to use it that way. We stay at this time because by our presence God wants to work salvation—both physically and spiritually in the lives of those around us.

May our Father continue to work in calling people to repentance and to receiving His divine gift of life.

Lee

In thee, Oh Lord, do I put my trust; let me never be ashamed: Deliver me in Thy righteousness. (Psalm 31:1)

My husband and I often visited the beautiful region of south Lebanon where endless citrus groves of lemon, grapefruit, and orange trees lined the roads. You could also see olive orchards and vineyards growing everywhere in this area the Bible calls "the Galilee of the Gentiles." In chapter 9 of the Book of Isaiah, the same chapter that prophesies the birth of Jesus, you will read,

> *Nevertheless there will be no more gloom for those who were in distress . . . but in the future He will honor Galilee of the Gentiles, by the way of the sea, along the Jordan.*(Isaiah 9:1, NIV)

This prophecy had appointed a future time when there would be no more gloom over the land. Today, however, the gloom still rests over its people, and they must wait.

It was also in this region where God had miraculously protected the prophet Elijah for three years from the severe famine that devastated Samaria. The Lord had directed Elijah to the house of a Phoenician widow in the village of Zarephath (presently called Sarafand) situated near the city of Sidon. She would obey God although she had only a handful of flour and a small crucible of oil left to bake bread and feed herself and her child one last meal before they died. However, because of her obedience to the prophet who requested that she feed him first, God continued to fill her jugs with oil and her jars with flour for the duration of the long famine. The story of her miraculous escape from the jaws of hunger and death is recorded in the Book of 1 Kings 17:7-24.

The Book of Jonah tells us that a great fish spat out this prophet on to dry land after he had been in its belly for three days and three nights. The Bible records how God had appointed Jonah to preach the message of repentance and salvation through the God of

Israel to the Ninevites, but he was so prejudiced—just as many are today—that he refused to obey and ran in the opposite direction. As he tried to make his escape on a boat, a storm erupted that would have caused it to sink. Jonah immediately realized that his disobedience was the reason for the storm and the pending disaster. In good conscience, he asked the crew to throw him overboard so they would be saved from God's wrath. However, Divine Providence had already prepared a large fish to swallow him and keep him alive throughout his *solitary confinement*. Thereafter, Jonah found himself on a beach. That event also took place on the shores of this region. For those who like to think of this story as a fairy tale, I would suggest they go to Matthew 12:40 and dispute the issue with Jesus because he said,

> *For as Jonas was three days and three nights in the whale's belly, so shall the Son of Man be three days and three nights in the heart of the earth.*

Jesus himself often visited this area and performed many healing miracles. In the Book of Mark 7:24-29 the story of the Syrophoenician woman is recorded. Disgusted with the hypocrisy of the Pharisees, Jesus left the village of Gennesaret and went to the vicinity of Tyre. It was there that this woman fell at his feet and begged Jesus to deliver her little daughter who was possessed by a demon. He tested her faith by saying some rather harsh words:

"Let the children first be filled: for it is not meet to take the children's bread and to cast it unto the dogs." (Mk 7:27) Her humble reply was, *"Yes, Lord, yet the dogs under the table eat the children's crumbs."*(Mk 7:28*)*

She had passed the test with flying colors, and the Lord answered, *"For this saying, go thy way; the devil is gone out of thy daughter."*(Mk 7:29)

Her faith gave her the victory that set her daughter free and the privilege of having her story recorded in the greatest book ever written.

How sad it is to see this land, so honored in Bible history with its stories of redemption, restoration, and miracles, bathed with the blood of innocent children. I truly believe that just as the Bible has promised, there will one day be a new beginning for the land and its people. The olive orchards that were destroyed by the bombs will be cultivated again to give their harvest of the delicious fruit they bear, and the citrus trees will be replanted to blossom once more. Best of all, the joyful sounds of little children playing in the fields where no more cluster bombs and land mines remain, or contaminated soil resides, will be heard again.

As I pondered with a heavy heart all of these matters, I knew that I needed to take a break and let my imagination carry me back to happier days and to the memories of my youth. As I looked at some old photos in my family album, I remembered my times and conversations with Mom and Dad and with many of the people who influenced me and shaped my life. It seemed that they too had a story to tell.

Chapter 3

Walking Down Memory Lane

The righteous shall flourish like the palm tree: he shall grow like a cedar in Lebanon.
— *Psalm 92:12*

The year was 1913, and at the age of sixteen, my father immigrated to America from Lebanon to get away from Turkish oppression and forge a new life for himself. His four older brothers had already established themselves in Connecticut ten to fifteen years earlier while the youngest remained in Lebanon with his sister to care for his parents.

Dad had hoped that his brothers would help him realize his dream of getting an education; however, that was not to be. Instead, they wanted him to start work immediately as a door-to-door salesman. Discouraged, Dad ran away to his uncle in Akron, Ohio, where he taught himself how to read and write English and then got a job on the assembly line at the Firestone Tire and Rubber Company.

Several years after father's arrival, he saw the Ottoman Empire crumble as World War I came to an end. That event led to the partitioning of the Middle East into mandates—another form of occupation—either to France or to England. Lebanon and Syria were handed over to the French while Palestine, Transjordan (present day Jordan), Iraq, and Egypt were mandated to the British.

The war that was meant to end all wars was now a memory, and in 1937, my dad decided to make a trip to Lebanon to visit his family. Resigned to his bachelorhood, Dad never intended to look for a bride; but as fate would have it, the matchmakers in his family introduced him to an attractive schoolteacher during the final days of his visit. It did not take Dad long to change his mind. Within one week, he and my mother were married in a Greek Orthodox church in Beirut. Thus, before returning to America, Dad found himself honeymooning for two weeks in Jerusalem and then Cairo. Two years later, I came on the scene.

As a teenager, I recall one conversation I had with my mother about her life in Lebanon before she married. Smiling, she confided in me her secret wish as a young girl before she ever met Dad.

"Back then, my dream was to marry an American who resembled Franklin D. Roosevelt, and as his bride, he would take me back with him to America."

Ironically, my father fit the description perfectly. Could it be coincidence? I think not. I call it answered prayer.

During my childhood, I remember how my mom would go to a little altar she had made in the corner of our dining room to pray before retiring for the evening. Each night she lit a wick that she placed in a small glass half filled with water and half with olive oil. Of course, the oil rose to the top as it was lighter than water, and it would continue to burn until morning when Mom would fill it again. Surrounding the light were three pictures or icons—one of the Resurrection, another of Mary holding baby Jesus on her lap, and a smaller icon of Mary and the child Jesus. She had purchased them all during her honeymoon in Jerusalem.

Mother was a woman of prayer; thus, she never let a night go by without talking to her Savior. Then she would come into my bedroom, pray over me, and tuck me in. She was also gifted with a beautiful voice and would often sing me a lullaby as well.

Throughout most of the years that she lived in America, Mother also served as a chanter in the Orthodox church we attended. She knew all the beautiful Byzantine hymns that were sung in Arabic and Greek during Mass. Years later, a priest, who had been newly appointed to pastor the church, decided to use an all-English choir and stop the traditional chanting of the hymns by a single voice. Sadly, he was not wise enough to integrate the traditional with the modern instead of simply canceling, to the dismay of many in the congregation. It broke Mother's heart, and a number of older people who were used to the tradition were sorely disappointed. Although a member of the new choir, I was still sad to see my mother's beautiful voice silenced from serving the Lord in church during the process of modernization.

Fourteen years passed before Mom returned to Lebanon to visit her family. The year was 1951 when my parents decided that it was time for me to meet the clan and spend at least a year in school there, learning Arabic. However, being separated from dad for such a long time didn't make my new adventure seem very appealing or exciting.

Mother, being fearful of airplanes, decided we would travel by sea. So one of Dad's friends graciously volunteered to drive us to New York harbor and to the pier where a ship was waiting to carry us across the Atlantic. Mom and I both cried as we embraced Dad, knowing that we would miss him very much.

The boat began to move, and we continued to wave goodbye until we could no longer see my father in the distance. With tears in my eyes, I felt more like a soldier going off to war rather than a happy voyager.

One of the stops the ship made before landing in Beirut was Naples, Italy. It docked there for one full day, giving us the opportunity of touring the city. I recall one of the ship's stewards advising everyone to purchase American cigarettes on board to use in place of currency for some of the purchases we would make. Most of the passengers as well as my mother did just that and, of course, went on a shopping spree.

Italy had not yet recovered from the aftermath of World War II, and you could buy almost anything with just a few packs of American cigarettes. That was all the vendors wanted besides American dollars.

Mother soon discovered that Naples was famous for its beautiful cameo jewelry, so with a few packs of cigarettes, she bought a necklace and matching bracelet from a street vendor. However, Mom did purchase a larger and more expensive cameo stone from a regular jeweler after haggling for ten minutes over the price. Just as in Lebanon, there was no such thing in those days as a *fixed price;* thus, when the vendors got hold of American tourists, they were considered fair game if they did not bargain. Of course, being Lebanese, my mother knew exactly how to engage in haggling; and the price went down. She was happy, and so was the jeweler. Mother also explained to me that Beirut had a superb jewelry district, and we would have the large cameo placed in a gold setting in Lebanon. I even recollect how inexpensive twenty-one-carat gold jewelry was in the Beirut market.

We finally boarded the ship by early evening after a tiring but fun day of shopping and sightseeing. The next morning we were on our way to Beirut.

I had grown up without ever knowing my grandparents, and now I would meet for the very first time my only surviving grandmother along with my Uncle Gaby and Aunt Malakie, Mom's brother and sister. Of course, I met the rest of the extended family who came to my uncle's house to welcome us. I also spent the year making new friends and learning, not only Arabic, but French as well.

I will never forget the day Mom decided we should visit Dad's home village of Niha. We had only been in Beirut for one week, and we were now going up to the mountains. A short while after we arrived, my head began to throb, and I found myself screaming from excruciating pain. Mother immediately returned with me to Beirut and on to the doctor's office. He wisely advised her not to take me up to the mountains so quickly as I was not yet accustomed to an immediate change in altitude. He was right because shortly after the doctor's visit, my headache disappeared. We then began to visit mountain areas of lower altitudes before attempting a second trip to Niha. From then on, I never experienced a headache again.

It was a memorable time for us, but after eleven months away from home, we simply missed Dad too much to stay any longer. We had come to Lebanon on the *SS Independence*, and we would be returning on the same ship.

After leaving Lebanese waters, The ship headed south toward Israel to pick up some passengers from Haifa. A few days later, the ship's captain announced on the loudspeaker that a stowaway had been caught onboard. It seemed that a young Palestinian man was trying to make his escape out of Israel, and some well-meaning passengers actually tried to hide him for a while but to no avail. He was sent back to Haifa from Naples.

Back home, one of the many good things that evolved out of our trip was the recognition my school in Akron gave, not to my grades, but to the school curriculum I had followed in Beirut. The principal decided it was more advanced than theirs, so I skipped the eighth grade and went directly into high school. Strangely, I remember making very few friendships that lasted beyond my high school years. Perhaps the distraction of having guys around played a role in keeping interaction among girls a bit superficial.

However, during my stay in Lebanon, I made many friends at the Evangelical School for Girls I attended. It was located on a lovely hill in the center of downtown Beirut and even had a marvelous view of the Mediterranean from the playground.

The student body was a mix of Christians, Muslims, and Jews. In fact, one of my closest friends was a Jewish girl by the name of Fortunee, and we all got along beautifully. It was also a time when boys and girls were segregated all the way from kindergarten through twelfth grade as each gender went to a different school. It was quite successful because every student remained busy with his or her schoolwork rather than distracted by the *opposite sex*. To the delight of my parents, I learned how to read and write two new languages.

Each morning, after our class answered the roll call, we would march off to chapel for prayer and Bible study. I can never forget the day one of the most famous and noble women of the past century, Ms. Helen Keller, visited our school where she was the guest speaker at chapel. You could hear a pin drop as she told us her personal story of triumph over tragedy. This was a beautiful lady, perhaps in her '70s then, who was deaf, mute, and blind from childhood. Her handicap never deterred her from achieving success thanks to a wonderful nurse by the name of Ann Sullivan who sacrificed her time and talent for many years, teaching Helen how to communicate.

We could understand Ms. Keller clearly as she spoke although her voice did not resonate in the normal fashion. When question-

and-answer time came, all the students presented their questions in writing to Ms. Keller's companion. She would read the question to her while Ms. Keller placed the back of her own hand flat underneath the chin of the reader, and then would respond. She apparently understood every word through her acute sense of touch as each syllable vibrated. This stunning woman had accomplished so much in her lifetime. Being the first deaf-blind person to graduate from college, she went on to become a prolific writer, lecturer, and activist, traveling all over the world with her ideas. No doubt, she left an indelible mark on the life of every person who met her or heard her speak, whether old or young, and we were no different. I believe she became everybody's heroine at school that day.

After returning home to Ohio, I continued to correspond with several of my friends for a few years; and then it dwindled down to just one, a Muslim girl named Leila whom I saw again in 1961. We remained friends until she married and immigrated to Australia with her husband.

Initially, Dad wanted us to stay in Lebanon for two years so that I could learn to converse even more fluently in Arabic. He also wanted us to stay a bit longer because he was preparing a surprise for me. Dad was adding a new room to our house that would become my bedroom, but we arrived halfway through the building process. Nevertheless, Dad was extremely happy to have us back. His face appeared so tired and thin that it left no doubt in our minds we had made the right decision to come home earlier than expected.

Dad had hired an older gentleman, perhaps in his late '60s, to build the addition to our house. I could not help but notice that for a man his age, he had an unusually thick crop of curly-jet-black hair without a single white strand showing. I was certain ladies envied him his curls.

Our builder friend was of Lebanese origin also and quite skilled at his job. Dad soon discovered the best way to keep him happy and working diligently was to get him a small flask of whiskey now and then, his beverage of choice. Although never drunk, he did look very amusing drinking, singing, and working all at the same time. It took him another month to complete the job, and I finally had my own bedroom.

The years passed, and in June of 1960, I had completed my bachelor's degree at the University of Akron. After graduating, I worked for less than a year at the BF Goodrich tire and rubber company as executive secretary to the foreign marketing manager. However, my parents' intention of returning to the land of their birth after Dad retired would soon materialize; thus, I handed in my resignation one month before we left.

It seemed that nothing could deter Dad from leaving at the appointed time, not even his inability to sell our house. Instead, he gave a power of attorney to a lawyer friend who sold it for him eight months later. By then, Dad needed the money, and it came just in time.

As usual, Mom wanted to travel by ship. No airplanes! She had nearly packed the whole house minus the furniture in four big steel trunks that accompanied us across the ocean.

In September of 1961, we boarded the ship and were finally on our way. Once again, the trip was memorable. The boat stopped for a full day in Gibraltar, later on in Palma de Mallorca—an island that belongs to Spain—and finally in Naples for two days, giving me the opportunity to visit Rome. It would take us a few more days at sea before arriving at our destination.

Finally, we got a glimpse of Lebanon's magnificent coastline; and as the ship drew closer, we could see Beirut more clearly with the mountains framing the background. While the ship was docking in the harbor, my parents and I stood at the railing, looking for members of our family who would be there to meet us. We eventually saw my mother's brother, Gaby, and her sister, Malakie, as well as my grandmother who was confined to a wheelchair. Some members of Dad's family were also on the pier. We started waving frantically at each other as the ship slowly came to a halt. When my feet touched land, I could still feel myself reeling for the next fifteen minutes as if I were still on a moving boat.

However, after we disembarked, the one thing Mom and I never expected to see was my Uncle Gaby limping so badly. We knew that he had been hit by a car while driving his motorcycle to work one day; but we never were told that the surgery to reset the bones, which were broken below the knee, was not very successful. I knew that some of the tears Mother shed that day were not all tears of joy.

It was, nevertheless, a very emotional moment, which included a lot of Lebanese hugs and kisses. After the wet-eyed welcome was over, we were on our way to my uncle's house.

Several days later, Mom mustered up the courage to ask her brother why he never considered a second operation to reset his lower leg correctly. You could sense pain and bitterness in his voice over the accident that was a hit-and-run. He replied, "I don't intend to spend another year of my life on my back, waiting to see if they're able to reset it properly for me." That day, the subject was closed, and we never brought it up again.

We received many visitors over the next few weeks who welcomed us back. As things quieted down, I was ready to learn more about the land of my roots and its traditions.

During the days that followed, Uncle Gaby volunteered to give me a few history lessons on Lebanon. I was inquisitive, but decided

I had read enough history books in school; so for the time being, I preferred listening to someone expound it.

I learned that Lebanon was a republic that forged its independence in 1943 from the French. The constitution was written based on democratic principles and an unwritten pact that the president would be a Christian; the prime minister, a Sunni Muslim; and the speaker of the house, a Shiite. All other minorities were represented in parliament. Thus, every religious group participated in some level of government. The members of parliament were elected on a six-to-five ratio in favor of the Christians, who were the majority at that time.

After gaining its freedom, Lebanon began to flourish. There were brief periods of civil unrest in its short history after independence; however, beginning in the late '50s until 1973, Lebanon was in its prime. It was a free market economy, and I could find any American product I wanted. Interestingly, I was never out of Rice Crispies or Post Toasties.

These were wonderful times to be living in Lebanon. People were exceptionally friendly, the cost of living was extremely cheap, and everything you needed or ever wanted was available.

The majority of Lebanese were either bilingual or trilingual, speaking Arabic, French, and/or English; thus, you never had to worry much about communicating.

Sandy beaches, mountain resorts, luxurious hotels, as well as some of the oldest and best-kept archaeological sites in the region attracted tourists from all over the world. Having one of the best cuisines on the Mediterranean rim was an added boon.

Beirut had become a major center for commerce in the region, providing a banking system similar to that of Switzerland; thus, the '50s and '60s saw unparalleled economic growth. I had arrived in 1961, and life appeared perfect.

While living in my uncle's house, I had yet to acclimate myself to a different lifestyle, one that was much less stressful. These were the days when people took afternoon naps, and unless you owned or worked in a shop or business enterprise, you were home early. Two o'clock in the afternoon marked the end of the workday as all government offices and banks closed by then. Being a civil servant who supervised public road construction, Uncle Gaby was home by 2:30, and off he went to bed or the sofa for a two-hour nap. I never did get used to siestas during those first months. Since Uncle Gaby was a lot of fun to be with, and I had not yet made many friends, I chose him to be my companion for a while. So when he went for his nap, I would try to create some sort of bearable disturbance to make him get up earlier and take me downtown in his little 1956 Italian Fiat.

He took such pride in his car that he would shine it every morning and make certain no one had scratched it the evening before. If Gaby heard the slightest noise coming from the engine, he would immediately take it to his friend, an Armenian mechanic named Mehran; and of course, I would go with him to check it out.

I remember how Gaby would call me *khalo* in Arabic, which simply means uncle. It was a Lebanese tradition to reverse the status of your relationship by calling your nephew or niece *uncle* or *auntie*. This was a term of endearment, and not unfamiliar to me since my mother often called me *Mama* and my dad called me *Baba*.

I did not have a car to drive yet and would not have needed it since Beirut was full of cheap public transportation. Almost every taxicab driver used an older model Mercedes or Chevrolet because they were so dependable. There was, of course, the usual private taxi that was relatively expensive while the more common type was the "service" (pronounced *serveese*), which acted like a minibus by picking up five passengers on its way to some designated sector of town. That whole trip cost twenty-five Lebanese piasters or the equivalence of ten cents. You could not beat those prices.

Nonetheless, I was still ambitious and wanted to drive my own car. Dad, however, was not prepared to add that expense to his budget since we did not have an apartment of our own yet. Thus, I kept on nagging my uncle to let me drive his Fiat, but the answer would always be, no. After all, that car was his baby.

One day, he finally gave in to my persistence, but it was to be under his supervision. As he sat on the passenger side, he soon discovered I was quite a capable chauffeur, driving in exactly the same way as the Lebanese—smart and wild. Eventually I convinced him to let me drive solo.

The question that inevitably came up was how would I learn to navigate all of the many roads when there were no street signs that made any sense and no house or building numbers? It was incredible! People just knew where to go because they recognized a building by the name of its owner and not a number. You simply *knew* exactly as the citizens of Beirut did. There was the Hamra, the Ashrafieh, the Upper and Lower Basta, the Dora, and so many other districts that included the suburbs. I soon discovered that it was a very big city with a complicated road system.

I now had to think of an original way to familiarize myself with the streets, so I decided to drive to downtown Beirut and learn the roads from there. My teachers would be the *serveese* taxis that parked in specific areas designated for each sector of Beirut from where they picked up passengers. I would wait and follow a taxi to an area of my choice such as the Hamra. As far as I was concerned, this was far better than trying to read a city road map without numbers.

One might ask me how I knew if that particular taxi was going to the Hamra since there were no signposts. Quite simply, the driver would keep yelling, Hamra, Hamra until he either lost his voice or got enough passengers to start driving. Like many of the Italians I had seen in Naples, the Lebanese could also be quite vocal if that's what it took to get the job done. It worked just fine for all the sectors of Beirut that interested me, and lo and behold, I learned how to get around. I felt like Christopher Columbus when he first discovered America. He must have been extremely proud of himself . . . and so was I.

My next hurdle was to find a job. I had spent six months doing nothing but meeting cousins and relatives, visiting and being visited; and oh, how the Lebanese love to visit. They invited me to lunches, to suppers, and to the movies. I was given the royal treatment as though I were the returning prodigal son.

Then I started to get impatient and a bit jittery. I could no longer remain jobless. I had gone to college not to sit around the house and twiddle my thumbs, waiting for the next visitor or suitor to call. I also needed to help Dad out financially if we were to find our own apartment and buy a car. He was living off a $100-a-month social security check, and even in those days, that was not a fortune in Lebanon. His savings started to dwindle, and so began the search for work.

I soon discovered that if you did not have Lebanese citizenship, you could not be hired without a special work permit provided to foreigners. If you were a manual laborer, it was quite easy to get one since most Lebanese were highly educated and only sought prestigious jobs. Thus, when it came to an office position, a Lebanese national had priority over a foreigner. It would have been necessary to prove that I was more qualified than my Lebanese counterpart.

I was getting depressed and started to make life miserable for my parents as well, threatening to go back to the States if I did not find a way out of this mess. I was twenty-one years old, and I needed to work. I needed financial independence, but most of all, I needed to help Dad. I did not like feeling useless.

Then one day, while we were visiting family friends, a gentleman by the name of Mr. Nabih Dagher, who owned a retail carpet establishment on Hamra Street, asked me if I would take care of his business correspondence. He needed someone with expertise in writing business letters since he imported rugs directly from Germany where English was the preferred language of commerce. I had been a student of business administration, and writing such letters was a simple task for me. I was ready for any job even if it were part-time and the paycheck, small. I never despised small beginnings, and this was a start.

Ironically, his shop was on the street floor of the building where an American Baptist missionary lived with his wife and their two young sons. Being an Evangelical Christian himself, Nabih knew that Dr. Brown was looking for a responsible executive secretary who would take care of the office duties and business matters relating to the church and the mission he directed. Nabih asked me if I would be interested, and of course, the answer was yes. He introduced us and was kind enough to recommend me. After the interview, Dr. Brown appeared extremely pleased, and he hired me on the spot.

Along with being the pastor of an English-speaking Baptist church he founded in Ras Beirut, Dr. Brown was also studying for a law degree by correspondence. So besides my regular duties, I thoroughly enjoyed the task of reviewing and editing his case studies since anything pertaining to law interested me. There were no computers then, so I typed everything and sent it out by mail. Luckily, I was a very fast typist. I also wrote and edited articles on different topics for the monthly mission newspaper we sent to friends and partners who financially supported the work. I finally had a full-time job and a very pleasant one at that. It did not pay a great deal, but it was more than enough for us to rent an apartment of our own.

Dr. Brown also founded two other churches: one in the Arab sector of Jerusalem, and another in Alexandria, Egypt. In those days, Beirut was the center for many Christian missions in the region. It was also the only democratic nation in the Middle East with absolute freedom of worship. It truly was an island with a lighthouse in a sea of Islam.

I remember meeting Samir, the pastor of the Jerusalem church. This young man was born into the very tightly knit Druze sect that believed in reincarnation, and whose members dwelt mostly in the mountainous Chouf district of Lebanon. Their clerics possessed secret religious writings they never revealed to anyone, not even to their own community. However, they had no holy book of their own in the sense of an inspired Word of God. They simply used the Muslim Koran at their funerals or other religious ceremonies, and when it seemed convenient, they would call themselves a Muslim sect.

Samir's dad was a notable businessman in his community and quite wealthy. After becoming a Christian, Samir was literally disowned by his father. In spite of the opposition, he did lead his mother to Christ when she was on her deathbed as well as a younger brother. Having also dabbled in the occult before his conversion to Christianity, Samir recounted taking all the books he had accumulated on the subject and burning them. He had become a new man in Christ, completely set free from the stranglehold of the occult.

I also met Mounir, an upcoming young Lebanese pastor whom Dr. Brown had ordained. A brilliant student, he had just graduated from the American University of Beirut with a degree in chemistry but felt a calling on his life into ministry that led him in another direction.

Having ordained these two young eligible bachelors, Dr. Brown took on the task of trying to match them up for the purpose of marriage. Being single, I did not have to imagine for long the thoughts he entertained on the subject of matrimony on my behalf. He, of course, wanted to see all of his pastors happily married. However, I made him understand quite clearly but respectfully that I was to be kept out of that equation. Thankfully, Mounir had already met his future spouse at the university; and in less than a year, Samir met a beautiful Jordanian girl in Jerusalem who later became his wife; thus, the issue was laid to rest.

Dr. Brown never tried to pressure me into ever becoming a Baptist since I came from an Orthodox Catholic background. However, he did lead me to Christ in the sinner's prayer, and that was good enough for him. I attended many of his church services, and although he was an excellent preacher, I had to get accustomed to his loud style of preaching.

Dr. Brown's lovely wife, Shirley, and I immediately became very good friends. Sadly, one year after I began working at the church, she became seriously ill and had to go through a series of intense medical examinations in an attempt to discover what her problem was. The doctors, who were all specialists, could not come up with any plausible diagnosis.

One evening, I received a phone call from Dr. Brown telling me, as he sobbed, to come quickly to their home. Shirley was dying. I got down to my car as fast as I could and arrived to see the doctor at her bedside as well. Shirley's condition was very grave, but I could not believe or accept such a report. With tears in our eyes, we all began to pray and intercede for her as her blood pressure dropped, and the doctor could no longer get a pulse. Then suddenly, we saw Shirley open her eyes in spite of what first appeared to be a hopeless situation. God had marvelously answered our prayers that evening, and in that brief moment, he taught us how to live by faith and not by sight.

When she was able to talk, Shirley described how she had gone through an out-of-body experience. She felt herself rising and actually looking down at herself. Then she said to me, "Noor, it was such a glorious feeling that I didn't want to come back into my own body."

It seemed that she had been touched by heaven; and all the pain, all the heaviness, all the sorrow had dissipated in a twinkling of an eye for that one brief but beautiful moment. Thankfully, God, in his infinite mercy, had other plans for Shirley; and she passed the crisis. After her ordeal, she remained weak; and Dr. Brown, at the advice of the doctors, made the decision to return to the States permanently. It was a tearful time for all of us. I had only been with them for one year, and now we were parting company.

Before leaving, Dr. Brown wanted to make sure I would have another job immediately. He knew many of the administrators at the American Community School, specifically built to serve the very large number of Americans who lived in Lebanon and elsewhere in the neighboring region. He recommended me for a job opening as secretary to the bursar, and I was hired for the position two weeks later.

ACS, as it was called, taught a strictly college preparatory American curriculum. However, you could still learn Arabic as an elective. The school building was large and beautiful with quite a high student enrollment from kindergarten through high school. The school grounds lay below the rolling hills of the American University of Beirut that overlooked the Mediterranean with its rocky coastline. The view was mesmerizing. The building inside was painted white while some walls displayed wide diagonal stripes of red and blue. The work atmosphere was very pleasant, but never as pleasant as in that little office in the warmth of the pastor's home or in the church basement where I printed the mission newspaper. Those happier days would be gone forever.

All packed and ready to leave, Dr. Brown, Shirley, and their two boys prepared to depart for Beirut International Airport. I came with my car, as did Pastor Mounir who took over the leadership of the church in Beirut. We drove them to the airport and stayed until they boarded. With tears in our eyes, we prayed and said our goodbyes. They were on their way back home where Dr. Brown eventually became the pastor of a large Baptist church in Dallas, Texas, while Shirley continued on her road to recovery with God's help. It ended a period that impacted my life, and one that I would not soon forget.

Chapter 4

The Days of Wine and Roses

Thou art all fair, my love, there is no spot in thee. Come with me from Lebanon, my spouse, with me from Lebanon.
—Song of Solomon 4:7-8

The very first time I actually met my husband was in the summer of 1951, during our first trip to Lebanon. As custom dictated, many friends and relatives came to welcome us at my Uncle Gaby's home where we were staying. I was a chubby twelve-year old kid, and Roy, a scrawny teenager of sixteen. Being related to Dad, he came with members of his family to welcome us also. Of course, it was too early for any lasting impressions, and we never thought about or saw each other again until ten years later when I returned to Lebanon permanently.

A few months after my parents and I arrived in 1961, I had myself a few notable adventures with gentleman callers who wished to court me. In those days, when a young man was interested in a young lady, he would ask permission from the parents to call on her. If the young lady also appeared interested, then any exercise in dating required a chaperon, and that rarely occurred until things became serious. These were the *rules of engagement.* For them to actually go out together, an engagement ring was required; and a brother or some other member of the family would chaperone the couple to a restaurant, cafe, or movie. Of course, there were always the young rebels who might do things differently, but they were few and far between in Beirut society.

This was the Middle East; thus, if you have ever read the biblical accounts of marriages that took place during that period of history, they were all arranged. Such traditions remained pretty much the same until the turn of the twentieth century. However, with the advent of high tech communication, it became easier to mingle with the outside world. Thus the system began to wane in the bigger cities, but remained to some degree in many of the more rural areas, especially among the Muslim and Druze communities of Lebanon.

Just as Dr. Brown had affectionately tried to arrange similar meetings, my mother's first cousin, whom I lovingly called my Aunt Lorice, was an expert matchmaker. An extremely funny lady, she could recite the family history of every person she knew on her block—and the surrounding neighborhoods. Whenever she spoke to you about these people, she assumed you knew them as well as she did, even back to the generations that passed on long before you were ever born. Her conversation might go something like this:

Noor, do you remember Semira Haaj, the cousin of John, who lives two streets down from your uncle's house, whose mother died in an accident ten years ago after her husband Toni tried to commit suicide because she talked too much?

Lorice always kept us in stitches; thus, you could never get mad at her no matter how hard you tried. Even during the civil war, she could identify by ear every type of weapon that was being used, whether a missile or a rifle. She was one brilliant as well as funny lady.

I now had a full-time job with Dr. Brown and had moved with my parents a second time into a larger apartment. One day while Lorice was paying us a visit, she said to my mother,

"Cousin, there are two young men who are twins, and they're looking to get married. I want you and Noor to meet them, and she can choose which one she likes."

Mom tried to politely get out of the situation. "Lorice, I don't think that Noor is interested. She is working and very happy at her job."

Of course, Aunt Lorice never took no for an answer. When my mother told me what had happened, and that these two young gentlemen, whom I had never met before, were coming, all I could say in Arabic was, *Amirna la Allah*—which, loosely translated, means—Oh God, you take care of this situation. You'll always hear an uncomfortable sigh after that statement.

I didn't want to hurt Aunt Lorice's feelings, so I accepted to play her game. Luckily, I had an early dental appointment the day these two gentlemen were coming to visit. By nine o'clock, I was at the Starco Building where my dentist's office was located. The good doctor injected me with novocaine to numb the area, but apparently hit a nerve. It was not too long before the whole side of my mouth swelled like a balloon, and I looked gloriously gross.

When I came through the door of our apartment, Aunt Lorice and the twins, who turned out to be identical, were already there. I mused, whispering to mother, "Ma, how would I tell them apart on the wedding day? Should I marry them both just to make sure?"

She laughed as we made our way into the sitting room. The twins were shorter than I, but not bad looking; and as I turned

The Days of Wine and Roses

to greet them, they saw a balloon-faced monster. I smiled and tried to say hello but could tell my whole mouth was going in one direction. The shock of my demeanor shrouded poor Aunt Lorice's face with the look of having just seen a ghost, and I felt very certain that the twins received a bit of a surprise also.

After a short courteous visit, the two young men made their exit. Then Lorice began to scold me for looking so bad and not wearing any fancy duds for the occasion. I excused myself for the bad impression I had made, went to my bedroom, threw myself on the bed, and laughed in my pillow. They never came back again. Several days later, Lorice told me they had decided not to come courting because I was too tall; and after trying two more times to introduce me to some eligible bachelors, Aunt Lorice finally surrendered to what she assumed was my desire for spinsterhood.

Once when we were still living with my uncle during our first six months in Lebanon, I asked my dad to fib (may the good Lord forgive me) in my behalf because one gentleman caller simply would not give up. He had come from Australia, wife hunting, and saw me at my cousin's house. Unable to get it into his head that I was not interested, he kept visiting us repeatedly, hoping to convince someone what a great catch he was. My poor father had to suffer agonizing hours of superficial conversations with him just out of courtesy.

One day, as he approached the front door on his fifth visit, I ran into the kitchen and made my getaway through the outside kitchen door, leaving my poor dad holding the bag. I would have jumped out the window if it were necessary, but like most of the houses, the windows were barred with iron rods for protection against breaking and entering. I remained seated in the garden behind the house until he left. When it was safe to come in, I finally said to Papa,

"When this guy returns—and he will—tell him I'm engaged to whomever in Kuwait. Just make up a name and ask him to kindly stop calling." He replied, "But, honey, I don't know how to lie."

"Dad, it's just a white lie to stop him from visiting anymore. Do you want me to get physical and kick him out?"

Being a peaceful man, my father finally submitted to my devious little plan.

The next day, just as I had predicted, our friend from Australia came knocking at our front door; but instead of Dad saying I was engaged to some make-believe character in Kuwait, he got a bit flustered.

"Sorry, but my daughter is engaged—to Lieutenant Roy."

I was behind the bedroom door, listening to the conversation, and when I heard my father use Roy's name, I nearly fell through the floor. Roy was a real person, not some fictitious character. We knew every member of Roy's family and so did this gentleman. I began to vividly imagine my disgrace if they ever found out what I had done. So I decided I would bury my head in some hole like an ostrich and never let them see me again. Just as I had feared, our friend did pay a visit to Philip, Roy's brother. He went straight to his office and bluntly asked him if my engagement to his brother was a fact.

My little trick was exposed; and sure enough, the following day, Philip came for a visit, wearing a big curious smile. I felt so ashamed that my face began to turn beet red. I was so flustered that I never bothered to ask him what his reply to that indignant question was. I simply began excusing myself, trying to justify my reason for doing it. That was the bad part, but the good part was, the gentleman from Australia never did come back. It seemed that my dad had unwittingly given a prophetic word of knowledge to that gentleman, and perhaps Philip covered up my lie because in less than two years, I did wind up marrying the lieutenant. Life does have its ironies.

Ten months after my parents and I moved into a new apartment, Roy's visits became more frequent. Our relationship eventually got more serious, and he finally did pop the big question. Roy was not very romantic with words, unless in a letter; so his proposal was blunt, but sweet:

"How soon can you quit your job at the school? I'm sending my brother to officially ask your dad for your hand in marriage."

Smiling, I replied, "Soon I guess."

The following week, Roy came with his brother and with the wedding rings we had already picked. We placed them on each other's right-hand finger as tradition dictated. This sealed the engagement, and during the wedding ceremony, the priest would take them and place each ring on the finger of the left hand.

Having decided to get married at one of the larger Greek Orthodox churches in the eastern part of Beirut, it was going to be a big, fat, beautiful Lebanese wedding with five hundred guests. The invitations were ready to go to the printer when, to our surprise, Roy received orders that he was being sent by the air force to England for eleven months of special training. We began rushing madly to change the date of the wedding to an earlier one while preparing to leave for England just four days after. In the process, I drove my couturier crazy. Every time I went for a fitting, he would have to take in my wedding dress because I was losing weight rapidly. Finally, the big day in August of 1963, arrived, and we were married.

Back in 1958, Roy had already gone through pilot training in Great Britain by successfully completing the first course—flying propeller aircraft. During the second course on fighter jets, however, his career came to an abrupt end when the British government decided without reservation to fail all active non-RAF officers who came from the Middle East, including the Lebanese. He and his fellow pilots became the victims of a government's political ploy and policies. Sadly, they had to bare the consequences of the buildup of tension that began with the Suez Canal Crisis in 1956 when the Israelis attacked Egypt, forcing the British and French to intervene. Then it was followed by a short period of civil unrest in Lebanon. By 1958, the ongoing Middle East crisis ended up with the overthrow of the pro-Western government in Iraq. A lot of political intrigue, and as usual, the innocent paid the price. I used to tell Roy jokingly, "When they play the drums in Timbuktu, they make Lebanon dance to the beat and the tune." That was a prophetic understatement.

Roy's dream of becoming a pilot had been shattered. He experienced such disappointment and frustration that he was ready to resign from the military. He even told me about an Iraqi officer he had met who learned to fly solo by night after only one hour of training. They called him, the master of the cockpit, but he too lost his dream. As Roy went to hand in his resignation at the Lebanese embassy, the military attaché, after a long talk, convinced him to remain and change his career choice to signals officer and ground technician. It was apparent that the Lebanese government did not intend to pressure the British to reconsider their action, and Roy became resigned to his fate.

Once again, Roy would be going to England for more advanced technical training in less than a week after our wedding. Before leaving, however, Roy traded in his Sunbeam sports car along with mine for a brand new British Ford Zodiac that we arranged to pick up in London.

We finally arrived on a rather cloudy day in August. Thus my first impression of London was the dull dusty gray color of its concrete and granite buildings that seemed to mingle with the fog. It was not a pleasant image. However, my eyes finally did get used to the dreariness of the weather. In fact, after we finally settled into a house, I began to like England very much in spite of the lack of frequent sunshine that I had grown accustomed to in Lebanon.

Several years later, however, the dark gray buildings of downtown London all became the object of a major cleanup that restored the brightness of their original colors. Regardless of how dark the buildings were during our time there, I could never forget the beauty of the lush green countryside and landscape of England. The frequent rain and foggy climate kept the grass constantly green but of an indescribable shade I had never seen elsewhere.

After staying one week in London, waiting to pick up our new car, we finally were on our way to the town of Henlow where Roy would be stationed. We immediately began our search for living quarters only to find that there were no vacancies in the area. Roy's classes began the day after we arrived, and I had to stay by myself in a small hotel room for over two weeks until we finally received word of a house that was being vacated by its American tenants in the village of Hitchin, not far from the base. This was the miracle we were praying for. I simply could not have imagined myself living in such a hotel for eleven months, waiting each evening for Roy to return. It would have been a honeymoon nightmare, but thank God, our need was met; and we moved into a furnished two-bedroom house three weeks after we arrived.

It seemed that most dwellings in England had no central heating, and people used either their fireplace or an electric or gas heater during the winter. We also had a very old-fashioned natural gas stove in the kitchen with a meter underneath the sink and a coin slot where we put our shillings every time we needed to purchase gas.

The appliances we lacked could be rented, so the first thing we got was a twelve-inch black-and-white TV set. Luckily, the house had an attached utility room that we used as an icebox throughout the cold winter months. When winter was over, we rented a nine-cubic-foot refrigerator to keep food from spoiling.

Our landlady was a woman by the name of Mrs. Majors. She was extremely helpful but a bit antagonistic toward Americans and toward anything that was *foreign*. I could not help but smile when I discovered that she and her husband thought spaghetti was a foreign dish. Nevertheless, I did have the courage to tell her I thought spaghetti was an international food that everybody loved. However, I had to be very careful how I spoke if I ever compared something British to its American counterpart. I did not want to sound arrogant since this was her impression of Americans who had rented the house from her in the past. I learned my lesson the hard way when I innocently made a remark comparing the medical system of our two countries. She immediately lashed out at me with the words, "You Americans think you're so superior . . ." And all I could do was apologize. To keep the peace from then on, I simply avoided topics that might be controversial as far as she was concerned.

Eventually, I had Mrs. Majors teach me how to knit, using some of the most complicated stitches I had ever seen. Britain was famous for its wool; and its senior women, famous for how fast and how well they could knit, and Mrs. Majors excelled in that craft.

Three months had passed, and on November 22, we, along with other Lebanese officers stationed in England, were invited to attend a reception at our embassy, celebrating Lebanon's Independence

The Days of Wine and Roses

Day. We met many state officials of foreign countries, including the American ambassador. As we mingled with the crowd, enjoying the interesting company, we suddenly saw the U.S. ambassador jump to his feet, make a formal statement, and rush out of the reception hall. He had announced with much emotion and pain that President John F. Kennedy had been shot. His death was not yet made public, but the shock reverberated across the room, and everybody began to get up slowly and leave. The reception was over.

As Roy and I got into our car, tears began to swell in my eyes. We became even more agitated after turning on the radio to hear the newscaster officially announce the death of President Kennedy. We actually made a wrong turn and got on a wrong highway trying to get home. Hitchin was located just sixty miles north of London. It normally took us one hour to drive home, but in our confusion that night, it took us more than two.

Roy and I still found the news too incredible to believe. How could the president of the United States die on the day we were supposed to be celebrating the birth of a nation?

As we continued our drive home, my memory went back to another time and another celebration that suddenly came to an abrupt end, but the consequences were not of the enormity of that particular evening. It was New Year's Eve, the year 1961, and we were in the ballroom of the Officer's Mess in Beirut. My family and I were invited by Roy's brother, Phillip, who was also an officer in the Lebanese Army. This was the same place where we would eventually have our wedding reception one year and eight months later. That night, however, Roy and I entertained no such thoughts concerning any relationship, let alone marriage. He was, and intended to remain, a permanent bachelor—so he thought.

As the evening progressed, I decided to go out to the large ballroom balcony that had a magnificent view, overlooking the Mediterranean. Just across the street on my left, I could see the dazzling Phoenicia Hotel. Behind it would eventually reside the towering Holiday Inn with its luxurious theater that seated perhaps four hundred people. Sadly, these two hotels were devastated early in 1976 as the civil war escalated.

The '60s, however, were the days of wine and roses, and we were celebrating New Year's Eve—or so we thought. We were nearing the midnight hour, and as I returned to the table, someone on the loudspeaker system announced that all officers must return to their posts immediately while asking everybody else to vacate the ballroom.

That night, a group of men—one of them, an army officer—tried to stage a coup d'état to topple the government of President Chehab. They belonged to a party whose philosophy and goal was to create a "Greater Syria" that would annex Jordan, Palestine, Lebanon, and Iraq to Syria under one flag. It was short lived, however, and they were caught in twenty-four hours. Things went back to normal, but the result was one aborted New Year's Eve celebration. That would be my first and only encounter with an attempted coup d'état. Years later, I would live through circumstances that made this little fiasco appear like a Sunday picnic.

For newlyweds, this unplanned trip to England could not have been timelier. In fact, I felt that it was a wedding gift from heaven. Although Roy spent much time studying, we still visited many interesting places on weekends or holidays and attended a number of military functions on the base. We also experienced some miraculous encounters that we would never forget.

December came, and Christmas vacation drew near. Joseph, one of Roy's close friends from Lebanon, had gotten married a month before and wanted to spend his delayed honeymoon with us in England. Christmas break was only ten days away, and of course, we were more than happy to host the newlyweds. Having already planned for a road trip to Europe that would take us through Belgium, Germany, Switzerland, and France, Joseph and his wife, Hayat, were able to accompany us during our two-week holiday on the Continent.

We were finally on the road to Dover where we embarked on a ferry that took us, along with our car, to Calais, France. There was no tunnel yet, and it was extremely cold. Because the waters were very turbulent, I could not stay inside. I needed fresh air so that I would not get sick to my stomach from the heaving of the ferry. Roy and the newlyweds accommodated me, and we all stood outside; but I did pay a price by nearly losing my voice completely. I suffered from laryngitis throughout the whole trip and no longer could say much of anything. Thankfully, Joseph happened to be a man who loves to talk——a rare quality in most males. He was such a good storyteller that nobody missed my conversations. In fact, Joseph was quite an excellent singer as well, and he was not selfish in showering us with his gift as we drove through Europe.

Our first stop was Belgium by night. We found Brussels breathtaking with its Gothic and Baroque architecture—and its beautiful women wearing mink coats and mink hats to match. I had never seen such affluence before. I guess it takes big money and a lot of snow to bring out the mink, and there was plenty of both.

The next day as we walked through downtown Brussels, we asked directions from a number of people to the location of a statue called le Manneken Pis. We had heard so much about it from Lebanese who visited this city that we just had to see it. Not having done our homework, we assumed this was some gargantuan size statue; and quite naturally, we thought everybody in Belgium knew its whereabouts. As it turned out, most of the Belgians had never heard of it. Finally, we ran into one person who was able to give us directions. He chuckled and told us how to get there. After arriving, we understood precisely why he was laughing. It turned out to be a small nude statue of a little boy standing in the center of a fountain—expelling his urine in a dish. We all laughed and went on to see bigger things. Years later, that statue became famous, perhaps because of the many Lebanese who asked to see it. In fact, he now wears articles of clothing from a wardrobe the Belgian people graciously provide to keep the little fellow warm.

From there, we continued on to Germany in subfreezing weather. I felt my cheeks swell from the cutting wind, but I loved every minute of it. What protected me so well from the cold, however, was a real beaver coat that had been a gift from Margaret Metry, a dear friend of my parents. She had worn it for a number of years, and now she wanted to give it away. I was the lucky recipient back in 1960 when I visited her and her husband in Florida. I rarely wore it because it was so heavy, but it was perfect for this trip as it kept me cozy and warm.

The first item on our agenda was to purchase a German-made camera. In the city of Frankfurt, we soon located a camera shop and bought one we liked from a seemingly helpful salesman. Roy wanted one that was top of the line, and he willingly paid the price for it. But after returning to England, we discovered that this man of integrity had ripped us off by selling us a used camera in need of repair. Most of the pictures we had taken of our trip were half burnt. Had we known at the time that bit of news, it would have ruined our whole trip. Thankfully, we were ignorant of that fact, so now we were still happy and in a Christmas mood. Luckily, Joseph, the young groom, brought his own camera, and the pictures he took were practically the same as ours. He kindly gave us a set after we returned to Beirut; thus, the memories of that trip remained intact.

Interestingly, this camera salesman offered to direct us to a very nice yet inexpensive hotel in Frankfurt. Being naïve, we accepted, thinking he was such a kind fellow. Back in England, I concluded that our sly extortionist probably got commissions from the hotels he recommended, or he was on a guilt trip.

It was Sunday morning, and off to Cologne we went to visit its famous Gothic cathedral that still bore the marks of World War II on its walls. This magnificent structure became a world heritage site, possessing the tallest twin spires of any cathedral in Europe. As we entered, we could see only a handful of people praying. Sadly, it gave me the impression of being a museum more than a house of prayer. It had become an ominous example of the spiritual decline that Germany and all of Europe began experiencing after the war.

We even drove through the mighty Black Forest and played in the snow like little children experiencing their first snowfall. We also passed through Mannheim, a newly constructed city that sparkled at night like a brilliant sapphire with its Christmas lights.

Switzerland was our next stop where we visited the lovely city of Lausanne that lay perched on a steep hill. It was a perfect setting for our friend, Joseph, who not only had a beautiful voice but knew how to play the lute and the violin. So during our evenings in Switzerland, we all sat in the hotel lounge around a fireplace while

Joseph serenaded us with Arabic love songs. It was quite a romantic setting for two pair of newlyweds.

We took the opportunity to visit the village of Montreux, which lies on the northeast shore of Lake Geneva. My eyes became fixed on the tall majestically sculptured mountains in the distance.

The images brought to my mind the mountains of northern Lebanon. They too were majestic, particularly the ones that surrounded the villages of Ihden and Bsharre, the home of Lebanon's poet, Gibran Khalil Gibran. Approximately ten thousand feet above sea level, beyond these villages, a higher plateau cradled the famous Cedar Forest Reserve, and at its entrance sat a magnificent tree said to be more than five thousand years old.

It's no wonder that Lebanon is called "the Switzerland of the Middle East"; for they have much in common. Even the winter chalets that draped the mountainsides resembled each other. Above all else, they shared the grandeur of their mountains, and I was lucky enough to have seen and experienced both.

It was now time to go to Paris where we toured everything from the Eiffel Tower to the fabulous Gardens of Versailles. Of course, the Louvre Museum was absolutely breathtaking. It seemed you had to walk for hours on end, and you still did not see it all. Many of the paintings were extremely large and practically made you turn your head ninety degrees in order to view the whole scene, even from a distance. I can never forget the one depicting the defeat of Napoleon at the Battle of Waterloo.

Of course, like every other tourist, I wanted to look into the mysterious eyes of Da Vinci's *Mona Lisa* that seemed to follow me as I moved around her. This master painter had captured on canvas a mystical expression and smile that made me feel as if the Mona Lisa were alive and breathing.

We also visited a magnificent complex of buildings called Les Invalides where the body of Napoleon Bonaparte rests in a huge wooden sarcophagus. Our guide told us the story of how this became the final resting place of the famous general. In 1840, King Louis Philip brought back Napoleon's body from St. Helena where he had been exiled by the British and placed him in a chapel in Paris until the renovations on Les Invalides were completed. Finally, in 1861, his remains were moved to the most prominent area of the building under the huge central dome of the chapel. According to our guide, Napoleon, before his death, requested that they place his coffin, not in a vault, but in plain view one story below eye level so people who wished to visit his crypt would have to bow in reverence. It only tells you how pathetically arrogant man can be—even in death. It's a pity Bonaparte never understood that *God resisteth the proud, and giveth grace to the humble.* (1 Peter 5:5)

Our unforgettable journey was nearly over, and now it was time to go home.

Chapter 5

Miracles Never Cease

Deliver me in thy righteousness and cause me to escape: incline Thine ear unto me and save me.
—**Psalm 71:2**

In Paris, we dropped Joseph and Hayat off at the Charles De Gaulle Airport where they took a plane back to Beirut. It was now way past midnight as we continued on to Calais to take the ferry back home. My mother, an amazingly prayerful woman, never ceased to intercede for our safety, and that night her prayers would be tested.

Roy had driven most of the way, and I wanted to help by offering to take over the wheel for a while. It was early morning and still dark. Roy hesitated, but finally gave in.

The road was covered with at least two inches of slick ice, so I did not drive very fast. Not realizing that I was a bit too sleepy, I dozed off for a few seconds; and as I opened my eyes, I saw myself getting ready to slam into a truck that appeared out of nowhere just twenty feet ahead of us. I screamed, "Oh, Mary, mother of God." I was Orthodox Catholic, and that was the first thing that came out of my mouth.

I tried to pump the breaks, but the car kept skidding at the same speed—it just wouldn't slow down. We were sliding on thick ice at forty miles an hour, perhaps into eternity. Then just as we were about to crash, our car came to an abrupt halt, as if on a dime, no more than an inch away from the rear of that truck. Oblivious to what was happening behind him, the driver of the truck simply continued on his way. I did not wish to imagine what might have occurred that night. As our hearts pounded, Roy hurriedly came out of the passenger seat, asked me to move over, and said in a quiet calm voice, "No more driving for you tonight."

I knew it was my mother's prayers protecting us as I imagined an angel standing between that truck and our car. We truly had experienced the supernatural.

A second miracle occurred, perhaps not as dramatic as the first, but very pleasant nevertheless. As the ferry approached Dover, my voice immediately returned to normal just as suddenly as it had disappeared during our initial crossing.

The winter months passed by quickly, and you could sense that spring was in the air. Since the weather was getting warmer, Roy and I decided to invite my parents to come and stay with us for the remainder of our time in England. They had never been to the British Isles before, and we wanted them to enjoy a season of travel with us through Europe. We decided to give them a tour of England on weekends, and then they would return to Beirut with us when the time came.

Roy was already planning on a two-week holiday after his training was over. It would be spent driving through the Mediterranean coastal countries of Europe and finally through Turkey and Syria on our way home.

My parents accepted our invitation and flew in to London two weeks later. We spent nearly every weekend sightseeing together.

England was never short on medieval castles, so a week after they arrived, we took Mom and Dad to London to visit the magnificent Hampton Court Palace. Between the sixteenth and the eighteenth century, this was home to a number of British monarchs, the most famous being Henry VIII. Our very knowledgeable guide not only took us to each of the palace apartments, the chapel, and the courtyards, but he shared many interesting bits of information concerning the private lives of its famous residents that one normally would not read in history books.

While touring the Tudor kitchens, we learned that King Henry had a ferocious appetite and often commanded his cooks to prepare him six whole chickens that he personally ate in one meal. Little wonder that his pictures reveal a man whose width nearly equaled his height.

As we walked through the exquisitely landscaped gardens outside the palace walls, I could not help but be amazed at the array of bright colorful flowers and the enchanting aroma that permeated the air. Its peaceful beauty was a sharp contrast to the dark history of Henry's gluttonous appetite, greed, and fixation on producing a son that caused him to behead some of his numerous wives. (Sounds like a sixteenth-century Taliban) However, that day, I preferred to leave such stories of ruthless kings behind and focus my attention on the large elaborate tapestries that had been hanging for over four hundred years in the entertainment halls as well as the works of art and the magnificent gardens that surrounded the palace.

Such a place carries the legacy, not of the notorious kings that ruled from its portals, but the unnamed craftsmen who designed and built it, inside and out; thus, becoming a memorial to their amazing God-given talents preserved for the eyes of posterity.

Mom and Dad also enjoyed the routine of everyday life such as shopping or spending time at home just relaxing. I'll never forget the day when my parents and I decided to drive into the village of Henlow to purchase groceries.

We had the habit of speaking to each other in Arabic whenever we went shopping, and as the three of us entered the grocery store, a man and a woman standing nearby overheard our conversation. Suddenly, the woman turned around and asked us in fluent Egyptian Arabic if we were Lebanese. As it turned out, she too was from Lebanon but had lived most of her life in Egypt; thus, acquiring the accent of that country. She soon introduced herself to us as Aida and the gentleman next to her as her husband, Fred.

However, the unusual background for this very interesting encounter with Aida had been set when Roy and I were still making our wedding plans back home.

We had gone to Niha, Roy's hometown, as custom dictated to invite the rest of the extended family to the wedding. My parents accompanied us and helped distribute the invitations among the relatives.

In the village resided one of my dad's cousins by the name of George, who was born mentally handicapped. This man's older sister, Marie, had simply vanished somewhere in England after World War II was over; and George never heard from her again. We saw him in one of the homes where we were giving out an invitation card. He approached us after overhearing our conversation about the upcoming trip to England and immediately remarked,

"My sister Marie lives in England, so please tell her to come and see me. I haven't heard from her in a long time."

Of course, it was next to an impossible request, and I replied,

"George, there are over twenty million people in England. How do you expect us to find her?"

"Oh, I know you can. Just tell her to come."

He turned around and walked back to his seat. We just smiled and forgot about it for a while. However, out of curiosity, I did ask my dad about Marie; and he told us that she had the habit of disappearing for years while relatives wondered what had become of her. As a young teenager, she and her widowed mother had already gone to Egypt to work, and George, who was left with his aunt, received very little news from them. Being mentally challenged, he could not read or write, so he did small odd jobs to survive while his aunt took care of him in her home.

In 1937, during my father's honeymoon trip, he actually located Marie and her mother working as seamstresses in Cairo. These were the days of King Farouk before a military coup toppled his monarchy. Then, it was not a sin to be rich, and a segment of that society was quite affluent as businesses flourished. Thus people from all parts of the Middle East and even Europe went there, seeking a vocation and a better life. Since Marie's father was dead, she and her mother had to seek out a decent living; and unlike today, Cairo was the place to go. Dad said he never saw anyone so happy to see him, and before leaving Egypt for the States, he did get word back to her family in Lebanon that she was safe and sound. This unusual story made me feel as though there was some kind of a spiritual bond that had formed between Dad and Marie. I began to think again about George's request, but then I said to myself, *poor guy, this isn't going to happen.*

Now back at that grocery store in Henlow, an odyssey was about to begin. My mother's eyes began to sparkle as she asked Aida if she had ever met a woman named Marie twenty years before in Egypt. I laughed a bit at her question, but to my surprise, Aida's answer was,

"Yes, I did have a friend named Marie."

I was still skeptical about this and said, "But Marie is a very common name. It could easily be another person." However, she and this particular Marie had left Egypt together on the same ship bound for England.

It was 1946, the war had ended, and they both had married British soldiers. But immediately after landing in England, they parted company. Having corresponded with Marie only once or twice after arriving, Aida never saw her again. Seventeen years had now passed, and she did not know if this could be the woman we were searching for. Aida's husband, Fred, a very friendly person and eager to have us visit, remembered that he had a picture of the four of them taken on the ship as they were leaving Alexandria. He hoped to find it among his memorabilia. We now had a way of identifying Marie, and my skepticism began to wane.

We set a time to pay them a visit the following day and were warmly welcomed into there home in Henlow. After drinking a cup of tea, Fred got up and brought us the photo he had found. As my father gazed at the figures in the picture, a huge smile began to form on his face as he said in amazement, "This is our Marie!"

George's wish just might come true, I thought. The next hurdle, however, would be to locate her. Fred recalled that Marie's husband came from a small village three hours away by car northeast of Henlow. Were they still there, or did they move? Would our search end in success or failure? We would soon find out.

Fred and Aida graciously offered to accompany us to this village for the search. There was no way of knowing what we would discover. The following Saturday, we picked them up quite early in the morning in our car. We had no address to go by, but luckily, Fred told us that each city or township in England kept a registry of all foreigners at the police station even if they later became British subjects.

Upon arriving, we immediately went to the police station and gave them Marie's full maiden name. As the officer looked through the pages of the registry, we eagerly awaited his response. I felt that he was searching at a snail's pace, but then we were too excited, perhaps too impatient, and he was a bit too British. He finally looked up at us and said, "Yes, there's a lady by that name in our registry, and she lives with her husband on King George Drive at this address."

You could have heard a pin drop. We were all beaming with excitement as the policeman gave us the directions to her house. I could hardly wait to see what surprise lay in store as we dashed off in our car.

We decided to let Dad go up to the door first while the rest of us stayed a short distance behind. The excitement mounted as we waited to see if she would even recognize him. I know that Mom and I were both praying she would be the one to answer the doorbell. Finally, a short lady did open the door, and we could see her look up and say, "Yes, how can I help you?" Dad replied, "Marie, it's me, Elias."

She appeared confused for a few seconds, but then broke loose with a shout, "Elias, my cousin Elias," threw her arms around his neck, and began to sob. As we all followed each other up to the front door, she welcomed all of us with hugs and kisses. She emanated a joy so incredible that we began to cry with her. Marie's husband was inside, and as she called to him, I can never forget her words.

"See, I told you I have a wonderful family, and that I was not some nobody you married off the street. I am a somebody!"

As she began to introduce us, he stared at each one rather dumbfounded. We seemed to have made a very favorable impression on him. He saw people who appeared very stylish by his standards—and with a brand new car. He welcomed us in, and of course, recognized Fred and Aida. We learned later that whenever her husband got angry, he played the little game of trying to break her spirit and self-esteem by calling her a nobody along with a few other words. However, we met her two teenage boys who loved her dearly. She had raised them well. A year later in one of her letters, she related how her husband had completely changed, and that he never called her *a nobody* again. Respect for Marie had returned to the household.

I think she was praying for us to come even more than George was praying to see her again. We did spend a wonderful day together and invited her to visit us in Hitchin before we returned to Lebanon. A few months later, she came and stayed with us for two days.

Marie resided in one of the poorest areas of England where salaries were extremely low. However, she and her family lived in a pleasant government-housing project. Being the breadwinner at that time, she was earning only five British pounds a week doing housekeeping, and her teenage sons worked part-time to keep themselves afloat while they attended school. That was not much money. To make matters worse, her husband could not maintain a steady stream of income. He would start one business venture, then fail; try another, and fail again. He had received a major head injury during the war, which apparently did not help his character flaws. Nevertheless, the shock of our somehow *powerful presence* seemed to have been used by God to straighten him out with respect to Marie.

Although she was a wise and frugal woman, I still could not fathom how she was able to afford doing anything outside of surviving, but she did. Marie was truly an amazing lady.

During her time with us, we had much to talk about, and as we spoke, I discovered that her faith in God and Jesus Christ never wavered in spite of her circumstances and the fact that she never had a soul to talk to about her troubles—until we came. Marie never stopped going to church and never stopped believing. She was a survivor with help from above.

Of course, we had discussed George and his desire to see her in Lebanon. In spite of her difficult financial situation, she gave us money from her savings to give her brother when we returned.

We all wanted her to visit Lebanon and stay with us whenever the time was right. She promised to come, and she kept her word. I had never met such an engaging and persevering woman. She saved for her trip from her meager earnings, and how she did it, I will never know. A few years later, Marie arrived in Beirut for a two-week visit, bringing with her a beautiful handmade English throw rug as a gift for our bedroom. She was always full of surprises.

Although she had many cousins and relatives in Niha, we wanted her to stay with us, and she too did not want to stay with any other member of her family. We took her sightseeing everywhere we could: to the great cedars of northern Lebanon, to the majestic Roman temples of Baalbek, the magnificent Jiita Caverns, and finally to one of the oldest cities on earth, Byblos, with its large crusader fortress—and from where we get the word, *Bible*.

She had seen many marvelous archaeological sites. Having left Lebanon at such an early age, she never had the opportunity to tour her own country, and now she would have many wonderful memories to take back with her to England. We also got together and bought her a solid gold bracelet to remember us by when she got home.

A few days after Marie arrived, we took her to the village to see her brother. He kissed her as though he had just seen her a week before. In his mind, the world was a simple place to live in, and life in general was even simpler. To him, it was perfectly natural that his sister came, and that we had found her among millions of people. To me, however, it was perfectly supernatural.

Psalm 27:10 became so real in this life-changing adventure with George and Marie.

When my father and my mother forsake me, then the LORD will take me up.

They both had lost their parents at a very early age, and they both had to fend for themselves. But there was a mighty God keeping his eyes on them, and he had answered each of their prayers by giving George the opportunity to see his sister again, even if it would be for the last time, and by returning to Marie the dignity she so richly deserved. God had truly given her *beauty for ashes* and *the garment of praise for the spirit of heaviness.* (Is 61:3)

We never stopped corresponding with her until one day, two years later, her husband wrote us a letter that said,

"With much heaviness and sorrow, I am writing to tell you that my beloved wife, Marie, was killed this week by a hit and run driver . . ."

As I read the letter to Roy and my parents, tears began to swell in our eyes. We all cried that day because we had lost a beautiful soul a bit too early. Her life had been hard, but now she was in a place where there were no tears, no pain, and no death; only joy and perfect peace. This was not the end of Marie's story. Instead, a new and more glorious chapter was being written in heaven that would have no end.

Chapter 6

My Life in the Beqaa Valley

The pastures are clothed with flocks; the valleys also are covered over with corn; they shout for joy, they also sing.

—*Psalm 65:13*

In June of '64, Roy had completed his training, and we set our time of departure from England to our new home in the Beqaa Valley of Lebanon for the first week of July. A month before, however, Roy received a letter from his brother, Philip. Knowing that we would be traveling by car, Philip warned us not to attempt crossing into Syria. It seemed that our northern neighbors were kidnapping Lebanese soldiers at random and holding them captive in their infamous jails without due process in retaliation for some political crisis that had suddenly erupted between the two governments. This truly was an ominous foreboding of things to come ten years down the road when Syria would eventually occupy the Beqaa Valley as well as many other regions in Lebanon.

We now had to modify our travel plans. Roy finally opted to drive through Europe to Greece and take a boat out of Piraeus harbor straight into Beirut, bypassing both Turkey and Syria. We did not have many options left on such short notice, and we had to find a ship that would leave within a day or two of our arrival in Athens.

After researching alternatives, Roy booked the four of us on the only passenger ship, called the SS *Lydia*, that had available space and was departing within the time frame we needed. I was delighted at the thought of taking this unexpected cruise besides touring Europe during our two-week holiday. This surely had to be the icing on the cake.

We had spent ten days visiting some of the best spots in Europe before we finally arrived in Athens. I immediately asked Roy to take me shopping for a bathing suit so that I could swim in the pool that I assumed was on the deck. We later visited the Parthenon and toured Athens for the remainder of the day.

The next morning, we set out for the harbor in search of the ocean liner that would take us home. When we arrived at the designated pier, I saw three ships docked in their separate stalls. As we drove toward the first one, I noticed how big and beautiful it was and joyfully assumed that this was our boat. But after getting closer, I soon discovered it had a different name—the SS *Ausonia*. "Ah, well," I said with a sigh, "perhaps it's the next one." Now the second ship was a bit smaller than the first, but just as regal. Once again I checked out the name, but to my disappointment, it was not ours either.

Finally, as we approached the third boat, I looked at my husband and said, "Roy, this can't be it! That's a dingy! And besides, there are sheep on the deck!"

We stood there for a moment gazing in disbelief at the SS *Lydia* as it stood there in its entire splendor—sheep, goats, and all!

"The brochure did not say anything about sheep!" Roy muttered under his breath, "Honest, honey, I didn't know this was the thing

I booked us on." We later discovered that this was to be the final voyage of the SS *Lydia* before it would be sent to the bottom.

The humor of the scene finally hit me, and I began to laugh until my sides ached. We boarded the boat with our car and prayed all the way that we wouldn't sink. The rumble of the engines was so loud throughout the whole trip that we could barely hear ourselves talk. After our "cruise ship" stopped in Alexandria, Egypt, to unload the sheep and deck passengers (those who slept on the deck), our prayers were answered, and we finally made it home. I thought to myself jokingly, *what an honor it was to have been one of its last passengers.*

Roy was already stationed at the Rayak Air Base located at the eastern end of the Beqaa Valley, the breadbasket of Lebanon. Now we had to move from his one-bedroom bachelor flat to a larger apartment.

We had returned during the summer, so we were able to enjoy exploring the region together. The vast stretch of the Beqaa valley was surrounded by the Anti-Lebanon mountains on its eastern border, separating us from Syria, and the Western Mountain Range of Lebanon with its very high peaks, on the other side.

Whenever we drove to Rayak from Beirut, we had to go through the Dahr el-Baydar mountain pass, and just before our descent into the Beqaa, our eyes would capture that magical moment when we first viewed the whole valley beneath. Nature would unleash a breathtaking panorama of vineyards and multicolored squares and rectangles of farmland, each piece carrying in its bosom the endless variety of crops farmers cultivated. We could stop by roadside vendors and purchase anything we desired from watermelons to onions and from grapes to garlic as each season gave us the delightful flavors of its good earth. I was introduced to many exotic fruits I had never seen or tasted before. That valley produced the delights of a king's banquet, and I could partake of it anytime I liked.

Living quarters were always available on the base for every officer assigned to that area. The French had built the older apartment buildings when they were still in control of the country and eventually turned them over to the Lebanese government when they withdrew from Lebanon. The traditional architecture of that era required the ceilings to be more than nine feet high, giving the impression that you were standing in some corner of a colorless cathedral. However, Roy and I became the Michelangelos that filled the space with the vibrant color combinations and décor that would bring life to a dull room.

I discovered a climate in Rayak so dry that I would have to put a large bowl of water on a hot radiator in our bedroom during the cold winter months to get a bit of moisture in the air while we slept.

All the rooms of our apartment were quite large, including the kitchen. Interestingly, each officer was also assigned an orderly who literally acted as a butler and performed all the heavy household chores. We were lucky to have had a soldier by the name of Toufik, who was also an excellent cook. He would help me in the kitchen anytime I needed him.

Two years after we moved in, construction began on new apartments to accommodate the growing number of officers and their families. Each building consisted of two stories with two apartments on each floor. These were centrally located within the confines of the base rather than on the street directly outside as our apartment building was. Seniority gave us the choice of staying where we were or moving to more modern premises. The idea appeared inviting at first, but then Roy and I decided we would stay put. Soon after the new apartments were occupied, I learned that we had made the right decision. As it turned out, the first tenants realized something was wrong with their hot-water system. When they switched on the water heaters to take a bath, nothing would come out but cold water, and so they froze. They all thought the heaters were defective—until they discovered that if the family on one floor switched theirs on, the apartment above or below would receive the hot water and vice versa. The plumbing fixtures had somehow been misconnected in this most unusual manner. We got an earful of interesting stories from our friends who suffered this unexpected surprise. Of course, they fixed the problem, but it took quite a while as Roy and I continued to take our hot baths anytime we liked.

These were the glory years of Lebanon. The cost of living was still cheap while commerce flourished and tourism was at its peak. Europeans and Americans working in Lebanon were everywhere, and they did not want to leave. Americans, in particular, found life so wonderful that many entertained thoughts of becoming permanent residents after retiring.

Although Roy and I were living far away from the hub and excitement of cosmopolitan Beirut, there was much to do in Rayak. We had become good friends with our neighbor, Colonel Falvey, the head of the British military mission team to Lebanon, and his lovely wife. There were also many official holidays (perhaps more than any other country in the world) and numerous occasions for formal gatherings that we attended.

During the midmorning hours of the day, a group of officers' wives would gather over a cup of coffee at somebody's house—a typical Lebanese ritual. However, I soon discovered that I did not enjoy the routine of morning visits, listening to the latest female gossip or to small talk about the clothes and trinkets they bought at exaggerated prices they said they paid to impress each other. I soon found myself withdrawing from most of these gatherings.

Although Lebanon had an extremely powerful Christian heritage, the deeper issues of life and the spiritual things that truly mattered were never a topic of conversation among the ladies. I was personally more interested in talking about political or religious issues. These were things that most women then did not think much about, and I was not yet experienced enough to know how to draw them into my sphere of interest or influence. Instead, I simply withdrew.

Perhaps if I had read the opinion of one the wealthiest men on earth, King Solomon, in the Book of Ecclesiastes concerning the futility of material things, I would have understood what I felt and known how to open up a different sort of conversation. Certainly some of his thoughts would have been interesting enough to discuss, and the very idea that "all is vanity" could make one reevaluate his or her priorities.

Located only fifteen miles from Rayak near the breakpoint of the snow-capped Anti-Lebanon mountains lies the ancient city of Baalbek with its huge Roman temples. It was so close to home that we were able to attend many of the Baalbek art festivals. The committee responsible for the programs was gracious enough to make available complementary tickets for military personnel and their families for a number of programs.

Among the ruins, an outdoor theater was constructed for each performance. The seats for the audience were set up in the great court where the Romans had built their pagan altars. Some of the most famous artists and symphony orchestras from around the world performed on the stage which was built high on the wide steps leading to the six remaining columns of Jupiter's Temple. Sadly, the rest of this gigantic edifice was destroyed by earthquakes over the centuries.

Every year, Roy and I attended the operettas that Fairouz, perhaps the most distinguished of all Lebanese singers, starred in. The highly gifted Rahbani Brothers not only composed the words and music to all her songs but wrote, produced, and directed the operettas as well. The three brothers were considered a family of musical geniuses.

During the fateful summer of 2006, however, all programs for the festival were canceled; all the tourists were gone, no more lights, no more sounds; and painfully, Fairouz, through her recordings, could only sing to a home audience in mourning. She had rendered many love songs to her beloved city, Beirut, and moved people to tears through her enchanting voice. You could not help but wonder how such a city, which evoked Khalil Gibran to write of its beauty, had become a labyrinth of smoke and fire. Some of his poems appropriately became the lyrics to the music composed for Fairouz by the Rahbani Brothers.

In the '60s, however, Beirut was very much intact—no bombs, no demolished quarters, and no fires burning incessantly. Mom and Dad had their apartment in Beirut, so we could always drive down and have a place to stay over the weekend or any time we wanted to visit.

My Life in the Beqaa Valley

Rayak was approximately two hours away from Beirut by car, and you had to cross a mountain as well as the Beqaa Valley via the Damascus Highway to get there. During the winter months, we sometimes could not go down due to bad weather and snowdrifts that would cut off the highway. We had to wait for the military or the civil defense to unblock it. There were several occasions when people became stranded, and because the snow flurries did not cease, they froze to death in their cars. Even nature claimed Lebanese lives, but nothing compared to what human hands had done and were still doing.

I can never forget how one day in the winter of '65, Roy suddenly developed a fever. Then strange reddish pimples began to develop around his neck and spread to his face and body. Immediately, I phoned the medical officer assigned to the base who passed by our home shortly before noon. He took a look at him and said, "Noor, I think Roy should go to the military hospital in Beirut because he seems be showing signs of some sort of blood disorder."

Roy did not wish to use an ambulance and preferred to go down by car. I was, of course, the designated driver. It was snowing heavily, and the radio newscaster had announced that the roads would be closed within a few hours. So I made him dress faster than you could melt an ice cube in boiling water. In ten minutes, we were ready to move. I was hoping that we would not be caught in some snowdrift, unable to complete our journey down safely. The doctor had scared me out of my wits with his statement; now I was on a mission to save my husband, and I took it seriously.

By noon, we were on the road, and I was speeding down the mountain where most people got stuck. I started saying my prayers, asking God to please get us down to Beirut in one piece. I was driving on ice that was quickly forming on the road. The thought of Calais and our notorious skid in similar weather conditions never crossed my mind, thank God. Roy looked terrible, but he was laughing at me for being so agitated and so vocally prayerful.

The trip did take us longer than usual because we met traffic, trying to beat the snowstorm as well. Not being the only ones on the road, I did honk my horn a few times, something you heard plenty of in Lebanon. Horn honking was a daily menu, and I had gotten used to it. I believed in the old adage, "When in Rome, do as the Romans do." I was not going to let any driver get the better of me; after all, I was on a mission.

We finally arrived at the military hospital and called my parents to meet us there. They wheeled Roy into a hospital room and immediately began the blood tests. Mom and Dad had to take a serveese taxi because Dad never learned to drive. In fact, he always walked everywhere or took a bus.

I recall trying to give Dad a few driving lessons shortly after I had gotten my own license at the age of sixteen in Akron. To his dismay and mine, he hit the gas pedal instead of the brakes and veered at low speed into a two-foot high retaining wall that surrounded a lawn. He became so angry with himself that he decided to end his career as a driver, and I became the family chauffeur from then on.

As we sat by Roy's side, waiting for some sort of news, we saw one of the doctors coming toward us chuckling. I thought to myself, *how could he be so callous as to laugh when my husband may have a serious blood disorder*. He walked toward me and announced, "You have a husband who is suffering from . . . chicken pox." I nearly dropped to the floor. Our beloved physician in Rayak had almost given me a heart attack with his projected diagnosis and made me drive through heavy snow just to have some doctor here in Beirut tell me my husband had chicken pox. I must admit it took me only a few seconds to start laughing with relief and to forgive our doctor in Rayak. After all, we did get a two-week sick leave. That was reward enough along with the fact that Roy did not have anything seriously wrong with him.

After spending three days in the hospital and another five in Beirut, we returned to Rayak where he continued to recuperate for the remainder of the time. However, a few days after we got back, some of his close officer friends decided to pay us a visit and play a practical joke all at the same time. Chickenpox was a baby's problem, so they wanted to have some fun. I later concluded they had been watching too many American movies where the bad guys would put on women's panty hose or silk stockings over their faces in order not to be recognized. Thus our three overgrown pranksters decided to go around the base that day, placing stockings over their heads before knocking on the apartment doors of their closest friends to see what the reaction would be from the ladies of the house.

I had just taken a hot lemon meringue pie out of the oven when I heard the doorbell ring. Luckily, I had placed it on a table near the entrance; and as I opened the door, the shock of seeing their horribly distorted faces took my breath away, and my voice just would not come out as I tried to call Roy's name. I simply stood there frozen. All you could see were a set of wide eyes and a mouth miming the name of Roy. When they saw me in shock, they all laughed, took off the stockings, and yelled, "Surprise!" Of course, I recognized them, but I had not yet regained my composure. As the last poor officer, who only accompanied the brood and refused to be a part of their prank, came in, he received a punch on the shoulder from me that sent him reeling back toward the steps. He laughed and said, "Noor, I was the only one without a stocking, and I get the punch? Mercy!" Once again, even in fun, the innocent pay the price.

They all got a piece of my mind and a piece of lemon pie for *bad behavior*. Had that pie still been in my hand, I could have thrown it into somebody's face. I cannot imagine what sort of burns that person might have sustained from a pie, still boiling hot, as it slammed into a nylon-clad countenance. Thank heaven it ended well on that particular day. After all, these were still the good times.

Chapter 7

The Gathering Storm

Thou which hast shewed me great and sore troubles, shalt quicken me again, and shalt bring me up again from the depths of the earth.
—*Psalm 71:20*

In May of 1968, after five long years, we were awaiting with much joy and anticipation the birth of our first child. We were starting a family, and nothing pleased me more than knowing my parents would soon be holding their first grandchild in their arms. However, dark clouds had already begun to hover over our personal lives.

Early in 1967, my mother was diagnosed with colon cancer and underwent two surgeries during her ordeal. The first was an emergency operation the surgeon misdiagnosed. Thinking it was her appendix, he operated only to discover cancer instead. He quickly removed the tumors in an unprepared intestinal environment and hoped for the best.

I was in Rayak when she became ill; and when I arrived, for some strange reason, no one told me of the diagnosis. My dad was sobbing and walking back and forth like a person who had lost his way. I knew something was very wrong, but my aunt and uncle took it upon themselves to keep her cancer a secret from me by creating another story, and my dad unwillingly went along with them.

A few months passed, and she seemed better. I was now coming down from Rayak more frequently and staying longer to help nurse her back to health. She was improving, but very slowly.

In the meantime, Roy received orders to go to France for six months of technical training on the Mirage jet fighter. The Lebanese government had purchased a small fleet of these powerful jets to strengthen the air force. Roy wanted me to go with him, but there was no way I could leave Mom as she was still so very thin and extremely weak. Roy also had been experiencing difficulty breathing whenever he was under stress, and now I had to let him go alone. How I wished that I could take care of my mother and be with my husband all at the same time. You start to imagine the impossible when you're in such emotional pain. We said our good-byes at the airport, and I returned to help my mother.

During the next three months, she experienced slight improvement. Afterward, Mom demanded that I leave for France, saying she was feeling well enough and promised me that her sister would remain with her until I came back. I finally gave in and made reservations to leave for Paris the following week. Mother could not go to the airport, so with tears in my eyes, I kissed her and said good-bye at home.

I had lost a good deal of weight myself, and when I arrived in Paris, Roy was there to meet me with a big smile; but he too looked so thin that I could barely recognize him until I got closer.

When I entered the building, I saw Roy standing behind the guardrail. As we embraced, tears flooded my eyes, and it took me a few minutes to regain my composure. Even then, I still could not stop thinking of the person I had left behind, looking so pale and thin. Once again I started to wish a part of me were back home, helping the one who had nurtured and blessed me by being such a godly, sacrificial friend and mother while the other part wanted to be where I was at that moment, with a loving and caring husband.

Before I arrived, Roy had started his training in Paris and now was completing the second part in Dijon, located in the district of Bourgogne approximately two hundred miles southeast of the capital. This was the city of the famed mustard by the same name, and we happened to be there during the yearly wine festival. Each passerby could sample the different wines at all the open-air booths that lined the streets where beautiful French-style apartments had been built so long ago. They still possessed the artistically detailed wrought-iron railings that were so typical of early French architecture.

We also attended an all-nation Folklore Dance Festival that the city of Dijon had sponsored that year. Roy and I were able to spend two unforgettable weeks together in this lovely place, and now it was time for us to leave. Within a few days, we were on the road for the four hundred-mile drive to his third and final destination in the south of France, a village called Mont-de-Marsan.

Roy had purchased a brand new Renault 4L that did over forty miles to the gallon. It was small but very comfortable and very fuel efficient. Being a popular vehicle, that particular model was seen everywhere in France; and as small as it was, you still could drive it long distances without ever experiencing fatigue. We loved it so much that Roy decided to transport it to Lebanon when it was time to go back home.

To save money, my husband and another married army officer agreed to rent a two-bedroom house together at Mont-de-Marsan while all the other Lebanese officers opted to pay a much higher rate in a complex of small one-bedroom chalets that were built near each other in a lovely wooded area. We were to share the expenses and the housework as well.

The arrangement seemed amenable at first since the house was quite large. However, a few weeks later after seeing a doctor for some health issues, I discovered that we were expecting a baby.

We had waited four years for this kind of news. That was the good part, but the possibility of a miscarriage was the bad. The doctor said I would have to stay in bed for at least two months while he gave me injections to help prevent a miscarriage. He even made me put ice packs on my abdomen on a 24/7 basis for several days until things got back to normal.

Rania, the wife of the other officer, began to display a self-centered attitude by refusing to help in any way; thus, she would leave the house in the morning and not return till evening. It seemed that Rania had gone through one very healthy pregnancy that produced a beautiful baby boy who was being cared for by her mother back in Lebanon while she was in France. She simply showed no concern or mercy for a friend who feared losing her unborn child. Ironically, several years later, I was surprised to learn from Rania, who now had three children, that she had to be confined to bed for nine full months throughout two pregnancies because she had experienced two miscarriages after the birth of her first child. It was probably coincidence, but I could not help but wonder if she had treated her friend kindlier in Mont-de-Marsan, perhaps she would have avoided this problem.

Roy was now forced to take a short leave of absence from work to help me through this difficult time; and for the next seven days, began to change one ice pack after another until he was about ready to drop. After seeing how his friend's wife was acting, he decided not to ask anybody at all to help and to move out as soon as possible even if it meant paying more. I, of course, agreed wholeheartedly.

In the meantime, I also learned that Rania had passed on a rumor among the wives of the other officers that I was making an excuse to stay in bed so that I would get out of doing my share of the housework. Once again, Roy took the mop and duster and started cleaning the house between the ice pack changes. Our situation looked more like a Charlie Chaplin movie, but at that time, it was not at all funny. We told the other couple nothing of our plans to leave and thought it best to surprise them.

After the seven days were over, we quickly packed our belongings and quietly moved into the complex where the other officers were now living. At least we had friendlier neighbors, and Rania did get the shock I hoped she would. After all, there was no longer anyone with whom she could share the expenses.

When we settled in, I joyfully thought to myself, *halleluiah, we're free at last*. We also made the decision to never let any of our neighbors know the real reason why we left the house since gossiping was never one of my favorite pastimes.

Yvonne, a lovely French woman, who was the wife of another Lebanese officer, visited me daily. She knew very little English, so I was forced to practice my French with her, and soon my speech began to improve. When the doctor gave me permission to start walking, she would accompany me arm in arm to make sure I would not take a fall during our slow walks around the complex. I looked forward to our morning trips through the lovely wooded area that surrounded the houses.

The three months passed by quickly, and the training was over. It was now time for all the officers to return to Lebanon. Roy made arrangements with his closest friend, Riad, to drive me to a nearby airport so that I would fly into Paris rather than drive in with him in our Renault. He was afraid that if I accompanied him on the long trip, I might be putting myself in danger of losing the baby. After all, we had waited four years for this day to come. Roy left two days ahead of me in our car along with all the other families, so I had to wait the seemingly endless hours in our apartment alone until Riad could pick me up a few days later.

With everyone gone, there wasn't a soul I could talk to just to pass the time away. I did not even have a book to read since Roy took most of the luggage with him in the car. The only thing that kept me company was the uncomfortable ticking of a clock that hung on the wall and an old newspaper. I felt as if the two days of waiting were an eternity.

Thankfully, departure time came, but poor Riad arrived at the apartment with such a terrible stiff neck that it made driving quite a painful ordeal. He also felt such a burden of responsibility that his question every five minutes in the middle of our conversation was, "Are you okay? Is the baby okay?" I kept assuring him, "Yes, yes. The baby is fine and kicking, just keep driving."

We finally arrived at the airport, and I boarded the plane for Paris. It was perhaps a little less than two hours later when the plane landed, and Roy was there to meet me.

It was Christmastime, and Paris glittered with bright lights on every tree that lined the downtown streets. We were returning to Beirut in two days; thus, Roy booked us a room at the Lebanese Foyer. However, he did not want me to fatigue from too much sightseeing, so our small trips around Paris were short and gentle.

The next morning, we drove to the Champs Élysées where several roads converge on the Arc de Triomphe, a monument from the Napoleonic Era. I was reminded that Emperor Napoleon III's name was carved on another monument—the rocky walls of the Dog River Canyon fifteen kilometers north of Beirut, commemorating a French expedition he sent to Lebanon in 1860.

On the other side of Dog River is an ancient Roman aqueduct, which until 2006 had become the backdrop for many theatrical productions and concerts. Sadly, the Israeli assault had produced a silence: no music, no dancing, nothing—just echoes of the past that were carved on the face of that canyon, creating a stele gallery of the many invading armies from the time of Ramses II, Pharaoh of Egypt, until the French in World War II. This was 1967, however, and things were quite different.

It was now time to leave Paris and fly home, but before we did, Roy took me to a delightful café on the Champs Élysées that served the biggest and most delicious croissants I had ever tasted. I would take the fond memory of that breakfast, along with the many extra pounds I gained, back with me to Lebanon.

As our plane landed at Beirut International Airport, Mom and Dad, along with other family members, were waiting to welcome us back. I was a lot chubbier, being in my fourth month of pregnancy; and mom—although quite shocked at my size—appeared so happy, awaiting her first grandchild.

Shortly after our arrival, Roy was temporarily transferred for a year to the Kleyaat Air Base in northern Lebanon, so we did not have to vacate our home in Rayak. We would be living just outside the second largest city in the country, Tripoli, where military housing was available in an area called Mont San Michelle. It was located on one of the rolling hills not far from the seacoast, giving us a lovely view of the Mediterranean. Nevertheless, I remained with my parents since I had already planned to give birth at a hospital in Beirut. It was only afterward that I moved to our temporary residence in Mont San Michelle.

Two months had passed since our return from France; and early one morning, as Roy was traveling north on his way to work, his car suddenly began to skid dangerously on a bend in the road. The seacoast was to his left and a ditch flowing with water bordered the side to his right. He was not far from the city of Byblos, located approximately thirty miles north of Beirut, when a heavy stream of water suddenly overflowed from the ditch directly in front of the car. This activity of gushing water made that part of the road very slippery. The car was now out of control as it made a 180-degree turn toward the seacoast and rolled on its back. However, at that point, the road was not level with the coastline. Instead, there was a thirty-five-foot drop, and as the car kept rolling, it returned to an upright position while falling off the edge. By God's mercy, although the shoreline consisted of nothing but a rough rocky surface with no sand or thicket in sight, the car somehow fell on the only piece of vegetation that slightly cushioned his fall as Roy remained in the seat. Had he landed on the rocks or been thrown out, it would have been a certain catastrophe. Nevertheless, the fall was still very traumatic, and Roy began to suffer unbearable back pain a few minutes later. Luckily, there were people on the road who saw the accident and immediately called an ambulance from one of the nearby houses.

It was still morning when Roy phoned and said in a low tired voice, "Hi, I'm back, but don't worry, I'm okay." Of course, his very statement told me that it was not okay. He was supposed to be at work, miles away from Beirut. I finally managed to get a short version of what happened as the doctor did not want him talking too much. He was phoning me from the military hospital just ten minutes away from my parents' apartment, so I immediately drove there.

The doctor was at Roy's bedside as my parents and I entered the room. He assured me that my husband was going to be all right, but that he had to remain under observation to make certain he was not experiencing any internal bleeding. Although there was no direct spinal injury, his back had taken a beating, causing him to experience a great deal of pain in that area for a long time. He was released one week later with a month's leave of absence and slept all that time on the hard floor of my parent's home just as the doctor had ordered.

Three months after the accident, our daughter made her debut. Everybody was elated, especially Mom and Dad with their first grandchild. Their attention was now completely focused on little Cici, the nickname they had chosen for her. She was her Grandpa Elias's little darling, and he made sure I changed her diaper every time she did her *number one*, as we called it. I was changing Cici thirteen times a day when paper diapers were not yet popular. It meant washing and hanging thirteen or more diapers out to dry every single morning. I finally convinced Dad that we could afford to let her do her number one twice before each change.

Five months after Cici was born, I received the good news that our second child was on the way. Thus it never would have occurred to me that we would not be spending another Christmas together as a happy family. I thought the dark clouds had passed, but I was so wrong.

Our baby was now seven months old and very much in love with her grandfather more than anyone else in the household. When he was around, nobody else counted. On December 17, only eight days before Christmas, we received the news that Roy's father had passed away at his home in the mountains. Being in my third month of pregnancy and my mother not that well, Roy refused to let me attend the funeral with him. Instead, he and Dad went alone. His two older brothers had already made the funeral arrangements. They too were army officers with many friends; thus, a large number of their comrades in arms would also be attending.

Roy and Dad prepared to leave for the village of Niha from my parents' apartment. As my father walked toward the door, Cici began to cry as she never had before; so Dad came running back and picked her up, hoping to calm her down. She frantically held on to him, refusing to let go as if she were holding on for dear life. With much difficulty, I finally separated them, but a strange uncomfortable feeling came over me. Why was she acting like this? She had never put up such a fight before, and I could not console her after he left. Like Cici, I began to wish Dad had stayed with us. She kept on crying and whimpering for several hours after their departure.

The funeral was scheduled for the next day at 4:00 PM. Early that same morning, my Uncle Gaby came to see us and then left for Niha. However, by six o'clock that evening, Gaby suddenly rushed into the house, grabbed hold of Mom's shoulders with tears running down his eyes, and before he could say a word, Mama said, "Elias is dead, isn't he."

His reply stunned me as the one word I did not want to hear came out of his mouth. He struggled to say yes as he choked through his own tears, trying to explain what had happened. I did not care what had happened. All I understood was that my beloved father was dead; and instinctively, I threw myself on the sofa, fearing for the well-being of the baby I was carrying. I could not stop pulling at my hair and screaming, "Papa, Papa." There was no consoling me, and I was caught between my anguish and the horribly deep pain that in a split second had gripped my mother. At that moment, I did not know how to control myself. I kept repeating the words, "Look after my mama. Please look after my mama." I was in no condition to give her any strength or consolation.

I do not remember how much time had elapsed before I picked myself up and rushed to my mother's side. I held her close to me as we cried in each other's arms. There was no beauty for ashes now and no balm for the deep wound that we both felt in our hearts. My dad had always been the family's tower of strength, and now, the tower had fallen. An emptiness I had never before experienced suddenly gripped my soul—not realizing there still was more to come. My uncle took me aside and told me that my husband, Roy, had suffered a head injury in the same accident and had been brought down to the military hospital.

This was a Lebanese funeral that had gone all wrong. Normally, custom dictated that the women would be in one room where the body lay while the men were in another, receiving the condolences first. Then the guests would move on to the other room, view the body, and pay their respects to the wife and other female relatives of the deceased. On that day, however, when the time drew near to move the body into the church, the men decided to wait outside for the bishop who was to direct the funeral. Inadvertently, they all stood under the concrete balcony of a neighboring building. The balcony was also surrounded by a four-foot-high concrete parapet instead of an iron railing. Unknown to them, this parapet had no steel reinforcements.

As fate would have it, the bishop was late in arriving; thus while they were waiting, the balcony gave way, sending the concrete blocks down on the heads of fifteen members of the receiving line. Many of the attendees said the music of the band, and especially the trumpets that played funeral marches, had been so loud that it must have caused vibrations powerful enough to send the balcony reeling, dropping its payload on the heads of the innocent. One concrete block hit my dad directly on the head from three meters up, and he died as they were moving him from under the rubble. Roy also took a hit which fractured the left side of his head so badly that he required surgery to remove the part of the skull that had shattered. Later that afternoon, he was in the hospital, fighting a new demon. All other remaining victims received minor injuries with the exception of one other officer. The next day, the story of the tragic accident made it into all the Beirut newspapers.

My uncle finally took me to the hospital to be with Roy, but I now felt completely numb. My face became lifeless, and the tears that were flowing stopped. I could not even speak. Roy was in a coma, but as I was standing near his bed, I heard a still small voice say to me, "Do not be afraid; he will live, and I have let Elias remain by his side until he wakes up." It was too hard to believe, but I knew what I had heard in my spirit was real. I was normally an extremely emotional person, but at that moment, a sudden calm enveloped me. I felt a peace about Roy's condition that could only be described as supernatural.

The doctor allowed me to see him for a few minutes, and then I sat outside the room while the physicians conferred with the top military personnel. They were discussing whether to send Roy and the other officer to France for surgery. The commanding general of the whole army was there, and he was prepared to do whatever was necessary to get Roy and the other officer, who was seriously injured, the best medical attention possible. However, they had also called in one of Lebanon's top neurosurgeons for consultation. He confidently marched into the hospital and said to the general, "I'll perform the surgery. There will be no need to waste time sending them to France. I know what I'm doing."

Immediately, they sent Roy in for a CAT scan of his head, and the terrible truth was there in the image. The other officer had sustained a smaller but more immediate life-threatening injury, so he was the first to go into surgery.

After that operation was over, the doctor ordered the nurses to wheel Roy into the operating room. That night, he had performed both surgeries successfully. When the doctor finally came out to talk to me, he said, "Your husband will survive, but he may not be able to function. We can't be certain about how well he will recover because he sustained a bad wound to the left side of his brain one inch deep."

As I listened, I did not cry; I did not even become agitated, which was so unlike me. That still small voice was there to sustain me, and I knew Roy would recover. I simply refused to believe the doctor's report.

My mother was now my fortress of strength, but she had begun to experience pain in her abdomen. Throughout our ordeal at the hospital, she kept her pain a secret as she came every single day to be by Roy's side for several hours while I rested. She had set aside her own personal sorrow and health issues to be near me and the son-in-law she loved so dearly.

It was several days after the surgery before Roy regained consciousness and opened his eyes. That day was God's mercy on two very tired and disheveled women. Even Dad's funeral was postponed for ten days while his body remained at the AUB Hospital morgue. Mom was the prayer warrior she had always been and continued to build up my faith that Roy would conquer the mountain he was facing.

Another five days passed, and Roy had not yet spoken a word. The surgeon, wanting to see if he could respond or recognize anybody, took me in each day and asked Roy if he knew me. He was barely recognizable with deep dark circles around his eyes and immense swelling below the white turbanlike band that covered his head. He said nothing, and for the next nine days, there was still no response. Finally on day ten, when they asked Roy the same question again, he responded by pronouncing my name, but with great difficulty. He had recognized me, and of course, the doctor was elated, and so was I.

After one month, they discharged Roy from the hospital to recuperate at home but mentioned nothing about rehabilitation. When they took the band off, it exposed his head with the scalp intact but without any skull bone on the left side where he received the injury. We now would have to wait for the plate they ordered to the doctor's specifications from France. Roy would need a second surgery to insert it, replacing that part of the skull they had removed. I did not dare leave him without supervision for fear he might fall or hurt his head. That area of the brain had no protection, and I was not prepared to take any chances.

I began to do the rehabilitation myself by teaching Roy how to speak all over again. The doctor had already warned me there would be a speech impairment along with forgetting any language he had learned when he was older. He also mentioned that Roy would retain the knowledge of his own mother tongue, Arabic. The doctor was right. Roy did forget to a substantial degree his French and English, but not the Arabic. He also was unable to do any simple calculations. This was a man who was brilliant at math and planned to get his degree in physics during his spare time. That dream had ended, and we were starting all over again on the long road to recovery that finally did pay off.

Several weeks later, Roy was admitted to the Barbir Hospital, a civilian complex, to have the plate inserted. Now the big question in my mind was if we would ever be able to return to some sort of a normal life without so much emotional pain and trauma. That question was soon answered.

The Gathering Storm

One day, after returning from visiting my husband at the Barbir Hospital, I noticed that my mother was experiencing a good deal of discomfort. Her abdomen was distended, and to my dismay, I learned that she did not have any normal bowel movement for a number of days. Something was critically wrong. I rushed her to the emergency room at the American University Hospital on a Saturday night I will never forget. My aunt and uncle had accompanied me. We soon discovered that weekends were never a good time to get admitted into a hospital. Like most medical facilities today, they suddenly become understaffed over the weekend.

That night, they kept her under observation. On Sunday morning the physician who was on call said mother needed emergency surgery as her condition had deteriorated. She could no longer keep her food down. Since she was not a patient of any particular surgeon at that hospital, we had to accept the one who was on duty that day to perform the operation. He explained the likelihood of scar tissue having formed after her initial surgery. This would cause an obstruction in the intestinal tract and meant she needed a second operation to unblock it.

To my shock, it was during this crisis I discovered her real condition. My aunt admitted that she had kept the diagnosis of my mother's cancer from me because she did not want her sister to go through any more surgeries. I became so frustrated and angry with her that I blew up in her face right in the waiting room. I had no part in the decision-making process and neither did my mother. In a bitter voice I said to my aunt, "I could have taken her to the United States and checked her into the best hospital. How did you dare do this?" She tried to justify herself, but it would not hold water with me, and now it was too late.

When the operation was finally over, the surgeon came out with a smile on his face.

"Well, we got it all, and it has not spread."

It sounded like good news until six days later when the doctor decided it was time to take out the tubes from her side. To our dismay, her wound immediately opened up, and fecal matter began to come out. The stitching had gone wrong. I soon realized that the combination of medical school and hospital could be lethal. This gentleman was not only a surgeon, but a professor of medicine as well, and here were his interns practicing under his supervision on my mother. Of course, he never admitted any wrongdoing, and now the doctor concluded that she was too weak to go through another surgery to correct the problem. Instead, he fitted her with a colostomy bag on a wound that was never prepared for such a procedure.

After three weeks in the hospital, she had lost at least thirty pounds, and all her strength was gone. No words could describe my pain. I loved her so much, and now I had to mask my heartbreak in front of her to keep her morale up; but inside I felt as if I were dying. I could tell in our moments of silence that she too was trying to hide her pain in order to be my source of strength.

Mom never stopped smiling, and when people visited her, she would be the one to keep them entertained with her encouraging remarks and stories. When I was able to finally bring her home, I created any way and every way to keep her comfortable and protected from the irritation of the plastic colostomy bag on her skin. I would be her nurse throughout her ordeal from then on. I would also experience the suffering and anguish of those whose loved ones had been incapacitated or had died because of the folly of some doctors or hospitals that only saw the patient as a statistic. Whether it is indifference or incompetence, the results are basically the same.

Having completely forgotten about myself, my pregnancy took a backseat to my mother and Roy's needs. I never went to my gynecologist from that day on until I was ready to deliver.

The Gathering Storm

Three months had passed, and I was able to nurse her back to where she could walk around a bit in the house and sit with us at the dinner table.

After my second daughter, Gloria, was born, I refused to stay in the hospital for more than two days so that I could go back to caring for Mom. The Almighty had given me extraordinary stamina or I could never have been able to complete the task that was set before me.

About five years prior, I had two dreams that blew me away. In one, I saw mother, pale and fragile, lying on a bed dying and my dad standing far away. Unable to come near her, he said to me, *Take care of your mother.* The whole atmosphere of that dream was frightening yet ethereal, as if we all were embedded in clouds. In the second one, I saw myself sitting on a couch as my mother walked toward me with a tray of food in her hands. Suddenly, she slipped and began to fall back into a deep dark crevasse, crying out to me for help. In panic, I used all my strength to reach down and grab her in order to pull her to safety; but I couldn't, and she disappeared out of my sight as I kept calling out to her. I woke up in a cold sweat as fear gripped me after each dream. I tried to put them out of my mind. I simply wanted to forget and believe that nothing bad could ever happen to my mother. I tried convincing myself that perhaps I had eaten the wrong kind of food that caused me to have such disturbing dreams.

Now my mother truly was pale and fragile, my dad was no longer with us, and I was taking care of her alone. The pain in my heart was sharp. I knew the emptiness she was feeling because Dad was not by her side anymore, especially when she was alone at night in the hospital. Now both my dreams were starting to make sense.

As I entered the door of our apartment with my newborn baby, I ran into mother's room and placed my daughter in her arms. She lifted her toward heaven and began praising the Lord with the words, "Glory to God! Glory to his Name." The beautiful voice that had once graced the chanter's seat in the Orthodox Church had now become weak, yet determined. She looked at me and said, "Please call her Gloria." As far as I was concerned, no other name could fit my little baby better than the one Mom had chosen.

As mother's condition deteriorated, my Uncle Gaby begged me to readmit her into the hospital. This time, it would be back to St. George's where she had her first surgery.

I was on the road daily. Roy was now home, so I asked my uncle and aunt to take turns staying with him until I got back from the hospital. Of course, the three of us also took turns going to my mother's bedside. Each time I called Mom on the phone before leaving for the hospital, I could tell her voice was getting weaker.

Ten days later, to my utter shock, I received a call at home from Uncle Gaby. My aunt had been alone doing some housework for her brother. When he came in from work, he found her lying on the bedroom floor. He was sobbing and begging me to hurry over because Malakie was dead. His house was not far from ours, so I left everything and ran all the way with tears in my eyes once again. In less than five minutes, I was there. I rushed to her side, and as I tried to hold her in my arms, I could see a blue discoloration on the back of her neck. I learned later from the doctor who checked her that she had experienced a massive stroke. I was beginning to think that God had abandoned us to some ugly trick of fate. How was I to tell my mother? How could I let her spill more tears? I dried my eyes, called her at the hospital, and told her that I would be late because my aunt was a bit sick and that I needed to check up on her. We immediately sent word to the rest of the family. They all came as well as the doctor who verified the cause of death.

I did not say anything to mother as we quickly began to make the funeral arrangements.

By early evening, I was at my mother's bedside, and the first words she said were, "My sister is dead, isn't she." Fate had once again dealt Mom a severe blow, and tears began to swell in her eyes. Once again, I was given the burden of consoling her. Now Mom's health began to deteriorate even more rapidly.

During my mother's final stay at the hospital, she had one more mission to accomplish. Her heart's desire was to see her brother, my Uncle Gaby, married. He was now fifty years old and had no one to look after him. With grandmother gone and now his sister, he was alone. He had decided long ago to remain a bachelor perhaps because of his limp, but now things were different. My aunt used to come each day to cook for him, and once a week she would take care of the housecleaning. With Malakie gone, Mother knew he would need a companion.

One day, Mona, a beautiful lady who was distantly related to us, came to visit my mother in the hospital. She too had been living alone, having lost both her parents years before. My mother's instincts were always strong. I believe she had a prophetic gifting that she never fully understood, but simply accepted. When she saw Mona, she knew without a doubt this was the girl for Gaby. I do not remember how she worked it out, but the obstinate bachelor and Mona became officially engaged in my mother's hospital room and were married shortly after her death.

As a child of five, I can never forget overhearing Mom tell my father of a prophetic dream she'd had that night. Dad had just read the headlines of the newspaper that reported the invasion of Normandy by our troops, a battle that was referred to as D-day. It was June of 1944, and in the dream, mother had seen herself in a beautiful meadow on a clear starry night, taking a walk while pushing me in a baby carriage. Suddenly the heavens opened before her eyes, and a huge white cross appeared in the sky. She heard a majestic voice as if it were God's, speaking in French, a language she understood. She was his chosen vessel to hear He had already given the victory to the Allies at Normandy and that France would be liberated. Not too long after that, the bloody battle was over. In May of 1945, Germany was defeated on the European front, and the instrument of surrender was signed on French soil.

I cannot recall the exact date, but sometime after her extraordinary dream, she and my father took me with them to visit some friends. They were all sitting next to the radio, getting ready to hear the evening news. My mother had just finished relating the story of her dream when to everyone's surprise, President Roosevelt interrupted the broadcast and began to give a speech in French, announcing to the world, in nearly the same words she had heard, that France had been liberated. They all stared at my mother in amazement. She was truly a gifted woman.

My last dream was now coming true, and without any hope short of a miracle for her recovery, I told my uncle I wanted to bring my mother home since I refused to let her die in a lonely hospital room. As he tried to argue with me, I soon discovered the reason he was so adamant about keeping her in the hospital. He actually thought cancer was contagious and feared for the baby and me. I looked him straight in the eye and said, "Uncle, you're so ignorant and fearful of this disease, and you don't have to be. But I tell you this; if my mama dies alone in that hospital, I will never forgive or speak to you again for as long as I live."

That got his attention, and we took her home where I was able to nurse her for one more week.

That final night, I found myself no longer able to stand up from the fatigue, so my mother's cousin, Emily, stepped in and hired a nighttime nurse to help me. I was too depressed and too tired to refuse. I went to my sweet mother's little prayer altar in the corner of her dining room and lit the wick just as she had done all her life. But that night, I would stand and utter a prayer that broke my heart in a way I had never experienced before. I would have done anything in the world to keep my mother alive, and I was prepared to take care of her even if she were bedridden; but I knew the personal anguish that she hid from me so very well, and so I whispered a short prayer that went something like this:

"God, I love her so much. She has been my friend and everything any girl could ever want in a mother, but if you will not heal her, please take her home to be with Dad. Don't let her suffer anymore."

Have you ever wanted God to say no to your prayer? In my selfishness, I did want God to turn a deaf ear, but little did I know how quickly he would respond.

I usually never left her side at night until she fell asleep. However, on that particular evening, the nurse remained with her, and my mother's cousin put me to bed because I was hardly able to breathe. They gave me a sedative to settle me. I just did not want my mother to see me in this condition. As I lay in the other bedroom directly next to hers, I heard her say, *Ya, immee, ya, immee.* She was calling to her mother in Arabic, and then silence. I thought to myself, *thank God she's asleep*. Suddenly I fell into the deepest sleep I had ever experienced.

Early the next morning, my mother's cousin, Emily, woke me up to tell me that my mama had passed away peacefully that same night. As I sobbed in agony, I ran into her bedroom and began to kiss her brow. I remember whispering, "Oh, Mama, I'm so sorry I wasn't with you. Please forgive me." My burden of guilt began to grow and then dissipate. I did not know what direction I was taking on each guilt trip. Without my really wanting to, I had released Mom into God's hands; and in his infinite wisdom, he took over. Now I had lost two of the most beautiful people in my life, my mom and dad, exactly ten months apart to the day.

Chapter 8

The Tsunami Hits

Save me O God, for the waters are come in unto my soul . . . I am weary of my crying: my throat is dried: mine eyes fail while I wait for my God.
—*Psalm 69:1, 3*

I had a precious new baby to take care of along with my darling Cici. I also took time out daily to sit and teach Roy how to speak and calculate math all over again. I became his mentor for the next six months.

Roy's oldest sister, Philomena, had sent her daughter to help me out for a while as I became overwhelmed with all the things I now had to take care of alone. Our home was still in Rayak, but Roy was on extended sick leave, and his military career was on hold. Eventually he was asked by the military to vacate our house in Rayak as it would be needed for another officer and his family. It was now up to me to do all the planning and packing alone.

We continued to live in my parents' apartment as my dad had wisely told the proprietor of the building to make the rental contract in Roy's name instead of his. Now I had to deal with two different sets of furniture. I opted to sell as much of it as I could in Rayak and keep what I had in Beirut. I made several long and arduous trips up to the air base with my uncle, trying first to contact people who would be interested in purchasing our furniture. I finally sold most of the large items and brought the rest of our personal belongings down to Beirut.

Roy was improving, and he now was able to function. The hard work had paid off, and his ability to speak had returned except he spoke more slowly.

Then the relatives started harping at me to move out of the apartment because they felt the memories would always be too painful for me to handle. That was not the case, and I did not want to move; but I foolishly listened to their advice because I had suddenly accumulated too many belongings and became the unwilling servant of the things I possessed. Thus began my search for a larger flat. It was difficult to find anything similarly priced, but I finally did locate a bigger apartment in the eastern sector of Beirut called Ashrafieh that could hold the excess baggage I now owned. Little did I know this move was the worst mistake I would ever make in my life.

Sometimes God speaks to us mysteriously through our circumstances; but instead of listening, we turn a deaf ear, believing that our circumstance was merely a coincidence. We were supposed to move into the new apartment on New Year's Day, but we had not yet finalized the signing of the contract. Suddenly both Roy and I came down at the exact same time with the worst case of flu—high fever and all—just a few days before we were to move out. We had to postpone everything until we both got better. Looking back, it was as if God were saying, *Don't leave. This is a much better place,* but I did not heed his warning. By early February, we were in the other apartment. Oddly, I never liked it from the beginning. It was

The Tsunami Hits

bigger than anything I could handle, and I felt uncomfortable. It was not too long after we moved in that my life was turned upside down by the consequences of that decision.

The house really was too large to take care of alone. Roy's niece, who was helping us, encouraged me to hire a live-in maid. In those days, nearly everybody had one, but I could not find a woman whom I could afford; so against my better judgment, I unwillingly settled for a young Syrian maid. I also yielded to the idea because my body was experiencing the effects of all that had transpired in my life up until then. Fatigue would set in more quickly, and I was on the road to a physical breakdown. Nevertheless, I tried to fight it with what little strength remained.

At the same time, the grapevine had it that the military commanders were preparing to discharge Roy because of his head injury. Now came the heavy task of trying to prove to them he was capable of going back to his post. Their doctors said he could not return to active duty for whatever reason. We would never have survived financially had they gotten their way. With a lot of prayer and much footwork, we began to seek the talents of a number of civilian psychologists and psychiatrists who could test him and verify the fact that Roy was mentally capable of assuming his duties. We now had official doctors' reports in our hands, and we fought their decision with the help of his brother who was the chief financial officer of the military hospital in Beirut. Finally, we were able to convince Roy's superiors that he was still an asset to the air force. It was hard and it was long, but we did win our case; and with the help of God, he was back at work.

At home, this new maid could barely do anything right but talk. I was very unnerved with her and became easily angered. I also had to find an older woman who could come in once a week and help her with the heavy housecleaning while she did the smaller chores. I found a sweet lady by the name of Marie whose husband had abandoned her. She was supporting herself and her children, doing housework; and she did an excellent job.

Roy's niece was still with us, so I never left my children with anyone but her if I needed to run an errand. I was never comfortable about having any maid babysit my children. Cici was two and little Gloria, who could now walk, was ten months old. Our lives, Roy's and mine, revolved around our children. They were the love of our life.

The maid we hired came from Syria, and her family belonged to a strange Islamic cult called Aluites. They had placed her in an agency called Adra Services, and the father would come every month to collect her wages from them. These people were extremely poor with very large families, and lived off the labor of their children. I never approved of having anyone that young in my house. But I was extremely tired, both physically and emotionally, and our finances were very tight—a perfect environment for listening to bad advice and making wrong decisions.

It was a bright spring day in June of 1970, just twenty days before little Gloria would celebrate her first birthday. I needed to buy material for kitchen curtains I was sewing, so I decided to go on a short trip to a nearby shop. The housekeeper had come and gone that day, and my baby Gloria was fast asleep in her crib. As I looked down at her sweet face and beautiful eyes with long lashes that curled up to her brow, I could not help but thank God over and over again for this precious angel he had given us. I can never forget the strange feeling that came over me at that moment as I said in a low voice, "She's too beautiful to be real." I did not want to disturb her, and so for the first time ever, I took Cici and Roy's niece with me because she too wanted to purchase something. I

The Tsunami Hits

told the maid just to keep an eye on Gloria and not to touch her if she woke up. She hardly ever cried and had the sweetest disposition of any child her age. I knew that if she woke up, she would play quietly in her crib.

When Gloria was only nine months old, I remember gently throwing a rubber ball at her from a distance. To my surprise, she caught it without blinking an eye. I looked at her proudly and said, "I know you'll make a wonderful sportswoman one day." But little did I know that my dreams for her future would never come to pass.

After we got back, everything appeared normal, except Gloria was awake; and Yusra, the young maid, was carrying her against my instructions. I scolded Yusra and demanded that she follow my exact orders from then on.

While in the kitchen, preparing supper for both Cici and Gloria, I could smell an unpleasant odor coming from the outside. I tried not to pay any attention to it as I whipped up their favorite meal, a powdered baby food called Cerelac. I prepared it right away by mixing it with milk, so I gave Gloria to Roy's niece to feed while I fed Cici myself. The whole kitchen now reeked with that hideous odor. I finally recognized it as being a highly toxic pesticide I had once smelled in Niha. Farmers would spray it on fruit trees to kill insects. I could not understand why such a pesticide was in a city neighborhood. The only plausible explanation that came to mind was perhaps some person had been silly enough to spray trees in his backyard to the extent that its odor had polluted the whole neighborhood.

Gloria, who normally ate anything you gave her, did eat all of her food; but Cici refused to put any in her mouth as she was a very finicky eater. I actually had to force feed her at each meal. However, for some strange reason I could never understand, I impatiently threw the dish aside. A bit angry that she had not touched a bite, I simply gave up feeding her—something I had never done before.

In less than a half hour, Gloria began to scream in a way that was absolutely chilling. I knew immediately there was something terribly wrong. I picked her up in my arms and ran out shouting for help. The owner of the building lived in the apartment below us with his family. One of his daughters, who happened to be a nurse, quickly responded to my plea and drove us to the hospital where she worked. It took us seven minutes, driving downhill at high speed to arrive at the emergency room. As we rushed in, a nurse came out and asked me if I knew what had happened to my baby. Full of anguish and tears, I replied, "I don't know! Just assume she was poisoned and do something." My response was partially correct; however, they did not respond soon enough as they had not yet confirmed what kind of poison was in her system. The emergency team tried pumping her stomach, but to no avail. As it turned out, this type of poison required an antidote. My day had now turned into a nightmare, and my baby was gone. There would be no celebrating her birthday, and we would not learn until one month later who the culprit was.

When we first moved into our new apartment, somebody had given me a powerful pesticide for some diseased plants I had on the balcony. I never dared open the canister after I read the label, and instead of throwing it away, I placed it on a very high shelf in the kitchen far and safe from anybody's reach—or so I thought. A few months had passed and I completely forgot about it. The ceilings of our house were nearly ten feet high, and you could never see the things you stored on that shelf without a tall ladder. Ironically, I never did put anything else on it, and the container was not apparent to the naked eye. Someone would have to intentionally climb on the countertop to find it. Whoever did this knew precisely what it was and had placed just a tiny drop or two into the baby food, not enough to make the powder sticky, but enough to kill my baby. The murderer then threw the rest of the can with what remained in it out the window into a nearby empty lot where the police found it later. That was where the horrific odor was coming from. This killer had succeeded in doing to my heart what nobody else could, and I was totally undone.

There is no greater pain to experience than the loss of a child. Grief was being heaped on me repeatedly, and I could no longer bear it, but Divine Providence had spared my oldest daughter. Had I forced her to eat the way I always did, her fate would have been sealed also. Now the police had to decide which of the two people, the little maid or the cleaning woman, could have possibly placed the poison into the Cerelac. They had already interrogated everyone who was present that day in our home. The evidence of any fingerprints was contaminated as I personally had opened the can of baby food to feed my children. However, I never understood why the police could not identify a set of fingerprints on the canister of poison they found outside, but they didn't.

Four weeks had now passed, and no news. Nevertheless, God stepped in a second time in his mercy so that the innocent party would come out of this unscathed. Only three days before the police told me they were planning to make an arrest, I had a dream that was bigger than life. I saw how I would catch the maid lying, how she would confess to me, and then how I would drag her out of the house and hand her over to the police. I woke up thinking I was hallucinating. It's impossible, I thought, that this little girl could do something so awful; and besides, she was too short to reach that shelf.

After waking up, I immediately told my husband about the dream, and he said, "Go and buy the maid some trinkets and a new dress. This might make her say something that will tell us what happened."

The police were still investigating, and I had not heard anything from them yet. I rushed down to a nearby shop, purchased a dress with some costume jewelry and gave them to her. This little act of kindness triggered a response.

The next day, while she and I were alone, this girl started bragging and saying things that tripped her up. She began to talk about a canister that had fallen from the top of that shelf all by itself—which, of course, was impossible. I then grabbed her by the shoulders, and said to her, "I know you didn't do it on purpose, did you. Just tell me what you did."

She spilled her guts out, and eventually, as things got hotter, a cruel smile began to form on her lips as she blurted, "I hate you, and yes, I did put the stuff in their food. I wanted them dead."

It was exactly as I had seen it in my dream, and the words, nearly the same. Roy was not at home just then to help me. Although I was shaking and sobbing at the same time, I dragged her out of the house as if she were a rag, and took her to the neighborhood police station. "There's your murderer," I said. "Get her out of my sight." She also confessed to them, and as the officer in charge saw me in tears, he said,

"Mrs. Ellias, you just saved a lady from being humiliated because we were going to go and get the cleaning woman and bring her to the station for further interrogation. Most likely we would have arrested her. Go home. It's all over."

You will never know how much I thanked God that night for having spared an innocent woman the pain and humiliation of being arrested. She probably would have endured a beating at the hands of the police as she pleaded her innocence.

The Tsunami Hits

I was caught in the cross fire once again; only this time, I had received a direct hit. My heart had no gaping hole in it. Instead, it was blown to smithereens. I can never forget my baby's funeral. As she lay in the casket, I wanted to grab her and hold her in my arms one more time because the pain of the emptiness, as I tried to wrap my arms around her in my imagination, was too great. I went home completely broken.

The following day, the priest of the Orthodox church where the funeral took place came to offer his condolences. Instead of consoling me, his words wounded my spirit even more. I can never forget what he said while smoking his cigarette:

"Noor, I knew your parents well, and now this tragedy. I can see how it could make you want to curse."

Then I turned to him in anger and asked a simple question.

"Father, can you tell me what would have happened to my baby had I not baptized her in water? Would she still have gone to heaven?"

"No, she would have gone to a place called limbo, somewhere between heaven and hell."

In my heart, I said, *if that were true, then I do not want to have anything to do with you, your church or a God who would make innocent babies go to such a terrible place because they were not dunked in some baptismal font.*

My spiritual breakdown had begun. To make matters worse, three months later, my Uncle Gaby, a newlywed of less than a year, died suddenly in his home of congestive heart failure—a problem that had developed from a lifetime of smoking five packs of cigarettes a day.

This time, I did not believe I would ever experience emotional healing. I went into a complete nervous breakdown, crying out of control, and no longer sleeping. I developed such severe insomnia that I began to collapse physically. The next three years would be the longest years of my life, full of depression and arduous trips to the psychiatrist who put me on heavy sedation to get my nerves to calm down. Early in my treatment, I was referred to a psychiatrist by the name of Dr. Moretti who decided to double the dose at night of a medication called Limbotrol. The first night, I took the two pills and went into a deep sleep that felt more like a coma than anything else. There were no other words I could use to describe this horrible sensation. When I tried to wake up, I could not open my eyes, move my hands, or speak no matter how hard I tried. I was conscious of what was happening around me, but I could not respond and actually felt as if I were dying. Barely able to breathe, I fought with all my might against this terrible state of uncontrolled deep sleep. Finally, I won the battle and began to open my eyes. The experience had been so traumatic that I went back to the psychiatrist early the next morning, expressing my disdain at his instructions; but all he could say was, "Well just go back to one pill in the evening."

Afterward, I sought the opinion of a number of physicians, and each one would give me a new set of pills until one doctor prescribed what he called a cocktail of drugs at a time when I needed hospitalization. Little did I know that I would become addicted to prescription drugs. Not that my addiction took me to wanting more; on the contrary, I loathed the control they had over me so much that I took things into my own hands and threw them all into the garbage. I decided to go cold turkey, and then all hell broke loose in my body. Unknowingly, I started going into periods of withdrawal that could only be described as if snakes were crawling under my skin and so much more. I tried to tolerate these intense sensations for several days until I could not stand them any longer. Reluctantly,

I returned to the doctor with my problem. He was shocked that I had suddenly stopped taking the pills and said to me, "Noor, you just can't do that with these drugs all at once. We would have to wean you off slowly, or else the withdrawal symptoms would be too awful to handle."

"Now he's telling me," I replied.

Back I went again to this terrible *cocktail* for another three months as the long weaning process began. The doctor finally replaced them with milder forms of tranquilizers for my insomnia.

I continued to experience intermittent crying spells, but never to the degree I had when my nightmare began. However, I was still on an emotional roller coaster that would remain with me for a long time. My healing would be very slow, but it would come.

Shortly after Gloria's death, we decided (this time without anyone's advice) that we had to move. We searched incessantly, but could not find anything within the range we could afford to pay in rent.

One day, I said to my husband, "If only we could move back into our old apartment where I was truly happy." The rent there was exactly what we could afford to pay, but in those days, it was extremely difficult to locate what you wanted since very few people left apartments they had lived in for years. This was due to a law that gave tenants the right to remain indefinitely. The proprietor had no control over the premises or legal recourse to make them vacate. In fact, the owner could not even raise the rent regardless of the cost of living unless the government approved a bill allowing for an increment. It was a rather unfair law from the days of the French mandate, which they eventually rescinded in 1990 for all new rental contracts from then on without making it retroactive.

The God of heaven, with whom I was angry for all my pain, who saw me throw his Book on the ground after the death of my daughter and heard me say, "If this is what you do, I do not want you in my life," had lovingly taken care of everything for us. What a gracious God we serve, even when we lay the blame for the action of others—or ours—on his shoulders.

To our surprise, one of our friends from the building we formerly lived in called us and said that an apartment might soon be available. The couple living there had gotten a divorce while the man continued to reside in the flat. He was now ready to move out. Since we were acquainted with that particular tenant, who also happened to be the son of the proprietor, we called and told him of our desire to rent the apartment. His answer was, "As soon as I know when I will be leaving, I'll call, and you can consider the place yours."

That was the happiest news I had heard in a very long time. We waited a few weeks, and the call came. Roy went down, signed the contract, and we were in our new home within three weeks. Living previously on the third floor with my parents, we now would be on the sixth—a different apartment but with exactly the same floor plan as the other. Just being in that building, however, was good enough. God answered my prayers, and I began to think that perhaps he was looking down on us after all and had not altogether forsaken us as I had imagined.

Chapter 9

A Bright Light in the Horizon

And ye shall seek me and find me, when ye search for me with all your heart.
— *Jeremiah 29:13*

In 1971, I was expecting a baby again; however, during my second month of pregnancy, I had a miscarriage. The loss devastated me, but my gynecologist said that this might have been a good thing because he feared the drugs I was still on would have produced terrible deformities in the child. He encouraged me not to try having any more children until I was drug free. I did take his advice, and it would not be until my system had cleared itself of all the medications the doctors had given me that my daughter, Sandy, would come on the scene. She was born two days after we celebrated Lebanon's Independence Day in 1973.

In 1972, however, I was still convalescing from my bouts with depression. I began to seek God once again, reading every book I could lay my hands on—from the Koran to Zen Buddhism—and finding no consolation. During my search, I came across a book entitled *The Zen Doctrine of No Mind* by an author whose name I can never forget. On the back cover, he had written these words. "You do not need a personal savior to get saved," and ironically, the author's name was Christmas Humphreys. I tried to read it, but it made absolutely no sense. I soon discovered there would be no real answers between its covers. That was an understatement because I never read such gibberish in all my life. It was so ridiculous that I felt pity for anyone who might take it seriously. If I had ever met this man, I would have advised him to call it *The Doctrine of the Mindless*. Eventually, I dropped it in a pile of other books marked for the trash bin.

I started reading the Bible again as Roy and I began visiting different churches to see if we could renew our relationship with the God whom I had received years before as my personal Savior. On that day, I had given my life to Jesus, acknowledging that I was a sinner in need of salvation, and that he had paid the ultimate price with his blood for my redemption. I had made him my savior; but in my ordeal, I had not made him the Lord of my life. Although I had turned my back on him, Jesus never forsook me; and he would soon be reminding me of this.

Our sitting room had a sofa from where you could see directly into a corridor, leading to the entrance of our apartment. One day as I sat there reading a book, the doorbell rang. Roy opened the door, and to my surprise, I saw him greet Dr. Brown and his wife Shirley. Overwhelmed with a sense of joy I hadn't felt in a long time, I jumped up and ran toward them. I started to hug them both with all my might. It was so very good to see old friends once again. As we all sat down, Shirley looked at me and said, "Noor, what has happened to our beautiful secretary? I hardly recognize you." She, of course, never knew what had happened to me. Shirley was staring at a pale face with eyes drawn from the tears that ran down like water from a broken faucet for so many years. She hugged me again as I tried to relate my story in as few words as possible. I never liked telling it because it brought back memories I was trying to put behind me.

It was then that Dr. Brown—with his familiar Texas drawl—said, "Noor, do you mean to tell me y'all went through this without Pastor Mounir and Elizabeth ever coming to see you?" He appeared a bit shocked and angry although I tried to make him understand it was no one's fault. I explained that we had simply lost touch with each other over the years; but Dr. Brown refused to accept it as a valid reason. He got up, called the pastor at his home, and after a short conversation said, "Get yourself down here, right now!" Roy and I could not help but appreciate the sincerity in his speech and body language—and his eagerness to make things right.

In less than a half hour, Mounir and his wife arrived. As we greeted them, Dr. Brown did not give us much of a chance to say anything more when he interrupted and said, "How come you never called my secretary and stayed in touch? Did you know the loss they went through? You could have been there"

Poor Pastor Mounir. It would have been a very humorous scene if it were not for the fact that Dr. Brown was dead serious. Nevertheless, I just had to smile at his passion about the whole thing. After all, he had a pastor's heart; and he didn't like the idea that the church was not there for us in our time of distress. We finally settled the matter and continued to reminisce about the wonderful days we had in Beirut.

From this encounter, a close friendship developed with Pastor Mounir and his wife. We got together for lunch and then started attending church in Ras Beirut before Dr. Brown and Shirley returned to the States. From then on, Mounir and Elizabeth visited us more frequently, and we became even more serious about going to church and reading our Bible.

One year later, I had read the Holy Bible enough to know that a loving God had been there for me all the time. I then asked to be baptized and join the church. Roy wanted to join as well, but he had to be more convinced about adult baptism. He was told all his life, just as I was, that his first baptism as a baby had sealed him as a Christian permanently. We were even told it would be a sin to get rebaptized for any reason. It took me a year and some practical Bible study to get over that stronghold of religious tradition in my life. Six months later, Roy decided it was his turn to do the same. By 1973, my emotional healing began as I finally became reconciled to a loving Savior.

Each summer, the church rented a campsite that belonged to a Swiss evangelical mission in Beirut for a six-day retreat that was open to every member and friend. It was located in the beautiful mountain region of Nabaa es Safa. (In Arabic, *nabaa* means a spring of water). Roy and I had already attended a previous retreat, and now this was our second. We all met at church and formed a caravan of cars along with one bus for those who did not have any means of transportation. By 8:00 AM, we were ready to move.

The Damascus Highway lay ahead of us as we started our ascent. It took us approximately one hour to arrive at the campsite that lay among the most magnificent and tallest long-needle pine trees I had ever seen.

The camping area consisted of a series of single-room sleeping quarters built to accommodate the elderly or families with children, and another large area for the tents where the other campers slept. There also was a church building, a kitchen, and a beautiful area of granite picnic tables that seated one hundred people. This was nature at its best.

Each morning at eight, we all gathered for a prayer meeting at the church. Then we took a half-hour break for breakfast and returned for the praise and worship service where the Bible was taught. In the evenings, a guest speaker who usually came from America or Egypt gave an inspiring message. Throughout the rest of the day, we had programs for the children and volleyball for the teenagers or for whoever wished to participate.

The mountain air was so fresh and pure that I only needed five or six hours of sleep. I would wake up feeling more energized than if I had slept for ten. Roy and I got up early each morning before our daughters did and took a brisk walk around the campgrounds. We could see the higher lush green-and-pink mountains that rose in the distance. The green was the color of the pine trees as their needles appeared to intertwine while the rock formations captured the pink hue from the reflection of the rising sun. The scenery was breathtaking, and you truly felt the presence of God.

As the week drew to a close, we were sad to leave such beauty and peace. A loving God had touched us all, and relationships were built.

Unfortunately, 1974 would be the last time, for a very long time, the church would have a retreat like this again. Later on, many of those beautiful trees were intentionally cut or burnt, and the buildings partially destroyed as Druze militiamen came and took the *booty*, stealing everything that could be carried or unhinged. Besides all the furniture, they stole window frames along with the windows. They also stole doors, kitchen sinks, faucets, fixtures, and toilet bowls. Anything that could be removed simply disappeared. Nothing remained but the bare concrete walls. This scenario was repeated many times over throughout the conflict by the various militias.

The once-beautiful campgrounds had become a war zone and playground for thieves. However, what they could not steal or destroy were the memories of the days spent in Nabaa es Safa and the Word of God that had penetrated our hearts.

The grass withereth, the flower fadeth: but the word of our God shall stand forever. (Is 40:8)

One year later, on a lovely spring day in April, we formed another small caravan with a group of friends from church and drove up that same road to visit friends in the village of Faloogha. The weather was absolutely beautiful and sunny. After a very enjoyable day, we started our journey back home, not knowing that something was waiting for us in Beirut. None of us were listening to any news on the radio. Instead, we were singing popular Arabic hymns and praising God in our cars.

As we entered Beirut, we noticed the police redirecting traffic. There was a huge lineup of cars, and we waited our turn to see what road we could take. In the meantime, we turned our radios on as the newscaster was announcing the incident that would trigger a full-blown civil war in Lebanon. It seemed that just a few hours before we arrived in Beirut, a group of men had stopped a busload of Palestinians and gunned them down. There were no survivors. We also learned that this was in retaliation for the four Lebanese Christians who were shot in front of a church located east of Beirut just hours before this incident; and now revenge became the order of the day. The skirmishes that began in 1973, were always restricted or put down—but this incident would tip the balance.

The singing had stopped, and instead, confusion set into each heart that had been rejoicing and praising the Creator. This time the turmoil came from without. My personal battle was practically over, and my enemy, defeated; but now a new kind of war was launched, and the bright light in the horizon started to grow dim once again.

As the civil war escalated, one of its early casualties was a member of our extended family, a young teenager by the name of Camille. He was only eighteen, but wanted to volunteer for his two-year mandatory service ahead of time. In fact, he visited us one evening, begging Roy to help him enlist early. Roy tried to talk him out of it, but Camille would not listen. This young man wanted desperately to finish his term in the army as soon as possible and get on with his life and college career, but he never made it. Instead, he died while on duty inside the Phoenicia Hotel. His body lay slumped on the steps that led to one of the floors. The hotel had received several direct hits from missiles sparking the fires that asphyxiated him and the other soldiers on that fateful day.

Sadly, the next evening, while Camille's mother watched the evening news, she saw her son lying dead in the ruins of that hotel. His face was still recognizable, and his mother would never be the same again. The shock and emotional trauma eventually took its toll on her health while Camille's sister became blind from the endless tears she shed over her brother. Many years later, the Hotel Phoenicia was rebuilt, and the memory of those who died for their country inside its corridors would be forgotten by the masses, but not by their families who still bear the scars of that awful day.

Chapter 10

Shattered Dreams, Broken Lives

Remember, O Lord what is come upon us: consider, and behold our reproach.
—Lamentations 5:1

I remember how the neighboring country of Jordan had expelled the Palestinian Liberation Organization (PLO) from its territories five years before in 1970, and how Lebanon, always in the cross fire, had to bare the burden of their fleeing civilian refugees. We already had more than 150,000 Palestinians in festering camps that grew out of the Arab-Israeli War of 1948. Sadly, along with these new refugees came their armed guerrillas. Skirmishes began to increase on a much larger scale, especially between the Christian militias that were now armed and the PLO along with their Lebanese and foreign allies.

In August of 1973, the Lebanese newspapers reported how Syria's dictator, Hafez al-Asaad, had declared that Lebanon and Syria were one country and one people yet run by two governments. Many took that to mean the Syrians were intending to annex Lebanon.

Roy was disappointed and angry as he saw the military being forced to take a backseat and do nothing. He once told me that in 1973, the commander of the Armed Forces of Lebanon was prepared to enter the Palestinian camps where turmoil had already started to give hints of a greater military confrontation. The army was still a force to contend with. However, the civilian government, headed at that time by Prime Minister Rashid Karami, would not allow such an intervention. Many conspiracy theories circulated among the population as to why he hindered the army from performing its duty. Whatever the excuse, it was a major tactical blunder. It eventually cost the lives of more than 150,000 innocent civilians along with three hundred thousand critically injured instead of the five hundred lives the military had projected to be the possible death toll—had they been permitted to do their job.

By the end of 1975, the whole country was plunged into an abyss. I saw the arming of militias on both sides being created and probably funded by the very outside forces who had the most to gain from Lebanon's destabilization: our delightful neighbors on both sides of our borders, and beyond. You could take your pick.

The ugly colors of sectarianism also were displayed, and people were targeted because of their religious persuasion. We lived in West Beirut, the name that had become an unofficial region rather than a directional signpost. This was where "Muslims" lived. This was where we lived and continued to live. Many Christians, however, who now feared for their lives thought it best to temporarily abandon their homes—furniture and all—to seek refuge on the other side of Beirut or in some mountain village.

Thus with each Israeli invasion, it kept the Shiia Muslims as well as many Christians who lived in areas of greatest tension constantly on the run for their lives. They in turn became occupiers of other people's properties, breaking and entering into any home they found empty of its rightful occupants. Sadly, they would be living in them for the next fifteen to eighteen years.

After things calmed down, many of these squatters refused to give the apartments back to their rightful owners until they were compensated since their own homes had been destroyed. This left another segment of society, the absentee owner and tenant, to become another kind of refugee.

A vicious cycle of displacement had begun. It would be in later years, beginning with 1990, that the Lebanese government would create an official bank for displaced persons where they were given a specific sum of money to start rebuilding their homes. It was a long process as some got more while others got less, depending on who they knew rather than what they needed. It was no surprise since political corruption is rampant all over the world, even in our own American society where we continue to see people who were victims of Hurricane Katrina in New Orleans still without a roof over their heads. Sadly, no country is immune to this kind of skullduggery.

The war was getting more vicious. I saw Lebanese killed by car bombs or a sniper's bullet—or simply kidnapped by an unknown group and later found dead under some bridge.

Roy could no longer come home although he was stationed only ten minutes away by car from our apartment. It would have been extremely dangerous as military personnel also became prime targets for kidnappers and killers from the various militias, especially on our side.

This was not a war with any logical objective in mind except to destabilize and destroy. Many of the fighters were mercenaries without a cause. They were killing just to kill, given arms and ammunition by some unknown outside party, and getting paid to do it.

I lived with two children on the sixth floor where electricity was cut off for most of the day. We would listen to the news to find out when our turn came to have electricity so we could sneak out and buy food, perhaps gasoline and other necessities for our family.

With Roy no longer able to cross the green line to come home, I found myself and the children alone except for a very brief period when a dear friend from church by the name of Renee came to stay with me and help with the children. She remained for three weeks although she was planning to stay longer.

I'll never forget the day Renee, the children, and I attempted to make a trip to the bakery for some bread. After a period of sporadic fighting and small rocket exchange, things quieted down enough for us to get to my car. I said a short prayer, and off we went in my silver-gray Volkswagen Beatle.

The bakery was about a mile away, and as I began to look for a spot to park, a building in front of us took a direct hit on its roof from a rocket. I quickly turned my car around and drove at such a high speed that I was back home before I could count to ten. My oldest daughter, who was now seven, ran like the wind toward our building. I grabbed Sandy, and we all rushed up six flights of stairs to the safety of our apartment. There would be many close calls such as that, and a few that were even more dangerous.

During one of the cease-fires that was declared, Renee thought she would slip away for an hour to visit a friend who lived a short distance from our apartment. After she arrived, her friend's dog, for some unknown reason, attacked Renee from behind and gave her a big bite in her buttock. Her sitting time would be over for a while. She called me and explained her friend was taking her to the hospital to be treated for the injury while the dog was kept under observation to be certain he did not have rabies. Of course, Renee was never able to return. She went home to recuperate, and that was the end of my helper's time with me.

Eventually, our elevator broke down permanently, and I would have to carry everything—no matter how heavy—up to our apartment. Roy still could not come home. Sometimes there would be a grocery boy to help me, but most of the time, I had to carry everything myself. Life was becoming much more difficult. It was 1976 and one of the worst years of the civil war. The children missed seeing their father and so did I. We spoke every day a number of times on the telephone, but the children wanted their daddy home.

One day, I called Roy and told him that we would be crossing the green line that separated East and West Beirut to visit him at his office. He did not like the idea too much, but I convinced him that the kidnapping of women had not started yet, and that we would be perfectly safe on the road. As I drove, I noticed that the traffic was light but moving normally as a cease-fire had been declared. We arrived safely and stayed with Roy most of the day. During that time, I had some interesting conversations with non-Christian officers that centered around the Bible and the Gospel. They thoroughly enjoyed it and were very open to listening.

However, by 4:00 PM, Roy decided it would be best if the children and I returned to the safety of our apartment. We still had to get across that green line where so many people were abducted by unknown militants and shot to death underneath the bridge.

As I got into the car, I could still see Roy and his friends on the balcony of his office waving at me. They all appeared a bit worried about us, but I thought everything would be all right. Their fears and my confidence were soon to be put to the test.

As soon as I turned down the main road called, Corniche El Mazraa, I could see that it was empty of cars. I also noticed to my right the Military Court of Justice building, and in front of it, a

Shattered Dreams, Broken Lives

young man neatly dressed hailing me down. I wanted to play it safe and stop rather than continue and perhaps get a bullet in my back. As I came to a halt near the curb, he drew close and asked if I would take him across to the other side because he had somebody he wanted to see in a hospital. I could tell he had no weapon on him, and he did appear very innocent and clean cut. However, I replied, "Can't you see the road is empty of cars, and it looks eerie? I don't know if this is a wise thing to do. I'm thinking of turning back myself."

"Please," he said. "I'm sure nothing will happen. I've got to get to the other side. I know we can make it together."

I looked at my two children who were in the backseat of the car and reluctantly told him to get in. I wanted him seated next to me just in case; and as we talked, it slipped my mind to ask for his name.

In less than a minute, we arrived at the infamous Fouad Chehab bridge where many people had been kidnapped and killed. Suddenly, out of nowhere, a truck jumped directly in front of us. They were coined by the media as *Hajiz Teeyar* (the Flying Blockade). These boys specialized in abductions and killings. This was the period of the war when they practiced *dabih ala el' hawieh,* which meant, butchered by I.D..

In Lebanon, all ID's have a citizen's religious persuasion printed on it; thus, no Christian would dare show his ID if he happened to be in the sector where the Muslims dominated any more than a Muslim would show his if he were caught in the Christian sector. People who always lived together peacefully suddenly became violent enemies; and nobody really knew why. It proved to me that religion without a relationship with God produces only bigotry and terror.

My hands were beginning to tremble as a bunch of gunmen dressed in sloppy khaki uniforms jumped out. One of them spoke with what I thought was a Palestinian accent, but certainly not

Lebanese. He began to ask us questions about who we were and where we were coming from. He also demanded that we get out of the car and show him our IDs. The young man beside me, who I felt certain was a Christian, replied, "I don't have one on me." The gunman then forced him out of the car. Now my fears turned to what they might do to him. Trying to get the attention of the gunman I said, "Please, he only wants to go to the hospital to visit a friend." He immediately interrupted me and yelled, "Mind your own business. First, you tell me who this man is."

I was now shaking badly and said, "I don't know his name, but I know he just wants to go to the hospital." The young gunman placed his head through the open window of my car on the passenger side that was now empty and shouted, "You people want to kill us, and now we're going to kill you. Get out of the car!"

As my voice broke, I replied, "Do I look like someone who wants to kill you? Please let us go."

I nervously began rummaging through my purse, trying to find my military ID. I thought it might put his little mind to rest if he knew who I was. Luckily, I never did find it because he might have put me to rest permanently.

Then I began to think, *oh God, who will take care of Roy and the children if they kill me? What's going to happen to my husband?* Suddenly, Cici looked directly at the gunman and gave a powerful scream, "Mamaaa," that could have cracked a chandelier. To my surprise, this guy looked at her and said, "Don't cry, little girl, don't cry. I'm not going to take your mother."

That day, God had used her to literally save my life, but I could not get them to release the young man who was with me. The gunman took one final cruel look at us and said emphatically, "He's none of your business! Get out of here before I change my mind."

I could do nothing but pray. My children were with me, and I moved on with tears once again filling my eyes—not for myself this time—but for that boy. I knew in my heart the life of this young stranger whose name I never knew would probably be snuffed out. We were all caught in the cross fire of hate and distrust. I wondered what mother that day would lose a son whose only fault was wanting to cross that damnable green line to visit someone at some hospital. I had lost a child to murderous hands, and I knew what this mother would soon be going through, whoever she was. Her life would be shattered, her dreams for her son broken, and I had played an unwilling role in this tragedy.

After arriving home, we wearily climbed the steps to our apartment. I was still thinking about that boy and sobbing. At that time, I had a wonderful Egyptian housekeeper named Fawzia who had lived with us off and on between her trips to Egypt to visit her family. She opened the door and saw me in tears. As she held on to my arm, I told her what had happened and then said, "If only I knew the name of this boy, I could have called the radio station and talked to Shereef El-Akhawi. Maybe he could have put out an alert and asked for his release."

I would listen to Shereef every day on the radio. He was a newscaster who now became a voice for the voiceless that were being kidnapped every day on both sides. Because of his work, some were lucky enough to be released while others were not, but he never stopped trying throughout the first several years of the war. This was a man who should have been given a medal for his untiring work on behalf of the victims of kidnappings and their families. I believe he was one of the unsung heroes of Lebanon in an era when lonely voices and acts of heroism for a just and humanitarian cause could not be recognized.

March, 1976, revealed even more ominous signs of things to come. Electricity was barely available, and it would be harder for me to get out and buy food. Sniping increased, and innocent civilians standing in breadlines were the targets.

At the same time, a group of Muslim rogue members of the Lebanese Army rebelled and formed their own private militia, calling themselves the Lebanese Arab Army. To my dismay, they had made their headquarters behind our apartment building. They were more of a nuisance than a real danger, and it did not take long for them to fall apart.

One day in March, a member of their group came banging at my door. I looked through the peephole and, seeing him dressed in an official army uniform, I opened the door. He looked at me and asked where my telephone was. I had no choice but to show him, and then he said, "We are removing all the speaker parts of every phone in this building just in case messages are being sent to the other side, so I will be taking yours."

I became angry with him, requesting that he not do this because I would need my phone to stay in touch with my husband. Of course, he ignored my pleas, took the speaker and left. I then said to myself, *Man, is he stupid. I have another phone that I can hook up and use just as easily.* However, I hesitated, and thought it best to be discreet. They could be monitoring phone calls and discover what I was doing, so I found another way to contact Roy.

Luckily, there was a very kind man who was one of the leaders of another Muslim political party—which later became defunct, perhaps because they never tried forming a militia. I simply assumed that his phone had remained untouched. I knocked at his door and told him of my dilemma. He laughed and welcomed me in to call Roy any time I needed as his wife and I were already friends.

Although Lebanese, he had a terrifically strong Syrian accent which apparently helped him a great deal in our neighborhood. He had lived in Syria during his younger years, and that too was an asset for him. I contacted Roy and told him that I no longer had a phone and to wait for my call each day.

That same evening, I heard God's voice so clearly in a heart whisper, telling me that my family and I must leave Lebanon for America as soon as possible. That thought never even crossed my mind before, but now it was embedded too deep in my spirit to ignore. I immediately called Roy the next day to explain what I knew God wanted us to do. Being a perpetual optimist, even when things were getting worse, Roy could only remark,

"But, Noor, things have got to get better. Don't worry"

My response was so resolute that Roy knew I would not change my mind. The more he tried to be optimistic, the more I got angry. I finally said, "What do you want me to do? Throw myself off Pigeon's Rock for you to believe things will be getting worse?"

The Rouche, or Pigeon's Rock, as it is called in English, is a beautiful gigantic rock formation that lays approximately three hundred feet away from the coastline of Ras Beirut, one of the loveliest areas of the city. Many tourists enjoy visiting this masterpiece of nature that resembles a small chunk of Grand Canyon. Its high cliffs have often seduced master divers to try their luck at jumping. Unfortunately, there were also a few suicide attempts from there, so when I told him, "How about if I jump off Pigeon's Rock," (of course I was not serious about that part of my conversation) he knew that I was dead serious about our leaving. My prediction that the situation would get worse did materialize; and Roy, my persistent optimist, had to face reality.

Chapter 11

A Breath of Fresh Air

But God is faithful, who will not suffer you to be tempted above that ye are able; but will with the temptation also make a way to escape that ye may be able to bear it.
—*1 Corinthians 10:13*

The military establishment was in absolute chaos, and Roy wondered if it were possible to get an official permission for a long leave of absence. Being in the armed services, he needed that before he could ever get a passport. Roy finally went up to the Ministry of Defense, which was in the eastern sector, only to find it practically abandoned. Who could he talk to? Searching every office, he finally found an officer on duty who willingly gave him the permit without any questions asked. These people had been fully demoralized.

Situated only a block away from where Roy worked was the Office of the Sûreté Générale where passports were issued. This was his next destination. He put in his permission along with the application, and within a few days, he was able to get his passport from that same office. It was a miracle because a few days later, the Sûreté Générale received a direct hit and could no longer function. Roy had just made it in time.

The next step was to get the passport to me so that I could get his visitor's visa from the American embassy that was still fully functioning. He found a liaison man who was able to cross over with the passport and deliver it to me in spite of the terribly dangerous conditions.

The next day, I asked some Palestinian friends from church to drive me to the embassy. After arriving, the receptionist placed my name on a waiting list to see the person responsible for the visas. I eventually entered his office, gave him Roy's passport, showed him my American passport and all the papers that proved he was my husband. Resembling someone who had just eaten sour grapes, he looked up at me and said, "Where is your husband's permission from the Lebanese Military? I can't give him a visa without it."

I tried not to appear impatient. "Sir," I said, "my husband could not have even gotten a passport without the permission, so please don't give me any problems. I can't even see my husband right now, and you know the dangers of crossing. Kindly make an exception."

He responded in a rather sarcastic tone. "No . . . I need the permission."

Slowly, I turned to leave his office, and in a very low voice, said, "Thank you, sir, for your kindness." That day, he saw an angry woman leave and heard a thank-you that was more cynical than sincere.

Missiles were flying, and militiamen were sniping from housetops; a whole cocktail of delightful dandies, but I did get home and call Roy from my neighbor's house, asking him to send me his permission with the liaison who had delivered the passport. It took another wasted day, but finally his permission slip arrived, and off I went a second time to the embassy. I entered the same man's office and threw the paper on his desk. "There, sir, is your permission. Kindly give my husband his visa." He did not say a word as he stamped it. With a triumphant grin on my face, I grabbed Roy's passport and left.

Step number three was how to get out of the country. Roy had not received a salary for several months, and all I had at home were a few hundred pounds in Lebanese currency (approximately $75) that I had saved for groceries. How were we ever going to buy the airline tickets without any money? It had to be God's provision as we had no control over that situation. God told us to leave, and he would have to provide the finances to do it.

Several days passed, and while I was trying to get our house in order, Roy learned that all military personnel were to receive their back pay. God had wonderfully prepared the way and the means. Roy immediately went to a nearby travel agency and purchased our tickets. This left us with one thousand dollars in our pocket to get by on when we arrived. It was true that we were going to have Roy's sister and her husband meet us, and certainly, we could stay with them for a short period; but we still needed a long-term plan. We were leaving oblivious to what God had in store for us while we were in the States.

Another problem to solve was how to get to the airport. Roy hadn't been home for three months, and God had given me enough common sense and wisdom to discourage Roy from ever attempting to cross the green line to get home. There certainly had to be another way for him to meet us at the airport the day of our departure.

For safety reasons, military personnel were flown by helicopter between the Ministry of Defense located in Yarzi, four miles east of Beirut, and the international airport where they also had an air base. When I called Roy to finalize our plans, I asked him not to come home but rather to go up to Yarzi and fly down by helicopter to the airport on the day of our departure, and the children and I would meet him there. I was now the officer in charge, and Roy was taking the orders. After all, God had given me the directive, and I had to carry it out.

I cleaned the house and put everything important away under lock and key that I did not plan to take with me. I packed the luggage for all of us and gave a set of house keys to my pastor so he could put a young married couple there from church that needed a place to stay during our absence. It was much safer than leaving the house empty of any occupants. This would prevent anyone from attempting to break in with plans of becoming a permanent squatter. It was no longer just the refugees who were entering homes without permission. Many other less honorable people were taking advantage of the situation and doing the same. There was no police force to stop them. Pandemonium was just the order of the day, and you learned to live with it.

I had one final problem to solve; and that was what to do with our cars while away since garage space was not available in our building or anywhere else in the neighborhood. Auto theft had become one of the favorite pastimes of the thugs who roamed Beirut streets at night—and sometimes in broad daylight. Being paid and protected by the various militias, none of the scoundrels were ever caught. These territorial pirates would traffic the vehicles they stole into the Beqaa Valley and later, across the border into Syria. Thus Pastor Mounir suggested we rent space for our cars in the underground garage of the American University Hospital for the duration of our absence. Years later, in 1984, my silver-gray Volkswagen and Roy's white Mercedes that he purchased in '82 became prime targets, and both were stolen just a few weeks apart—never to be seen again. In fact, Roy's car was taken from him eight o'clock in the morning at gunpoint after dropping Cici and Sandy off at school. But at least in 1976, while we were in America, my Volkswagen and Roy's English Ford would remain hidden from the eyes of the thieves.

I had spoken to a gentleman who lived in our apartment building concerning the trip my children and I would have to make to the airport. He had connections with a Palestinian organization called the Saahqa and made preparations to have one of their men drive us there. These people had safe access to the roads in our area; thus, if we were stopped at any militia checkpoint, we could pass through easily.

April 16, 1976, was the day of departure. We prepared ourselves and got ready to lock up the house to leave. As I looked out the window, to my dismay, I saw something I had never seen before in Lebanon. The sky was cast in a thick yellowish tint created by a terrible sandstorm that had made its way into Lebanon from the deserts of the Arabian Gulf. It was near-zero visibility. I once again cried out to God and said, "Lord, you brought us this far. How can any plane land in Beirut now? Are we stuck again?"

I remembered that God had been right on time every time, so I mustered up enough faith and courage to make that drive to the airport. The Saahqa man had arrived with his car, and his Russian-made klashnekoff rifle. *What a combination*, I thought. I greeted him in quiet resolve as he placed our luggage in the trunk. We then got in the backseat of the vehicle, and off he drove at high speed.

The barrel of the rifle pointed upward on the passenger's side right next to the driver. Every time he would make a turn, that rifle would veer either to the left or to the right, depending on the direction he was taking; thus, my eyes were glued to that *klashen,* as we used to call it, throughout our harrowing ten-minute drive to the airport. I wondered if he would ever fly over some bump in the road that would throw the rifle in our direction. I began to imagine the trigger coming unlocked (if it ever was locked in the first place) and bullets flying our way. Of course, one's imagination can go wild under such circumstances, and mine did not take a vacation that day.

I sent up prayers to heaven for our safety, and we got there not a moment too soon as far as I was concerned. He dropped us off with our luggage at the entrance to the airport. I thanked him, of course, and off he went flying into the wild yellow sandstorm. There was no *blue yonder* anywhere in sight.

As we entered the main building, I could see Roy waving at us. We had not seen him for such a long time, and now we were hugging as Cici and Sandy kept kissing their father's cheeks until they turned beet red. It was a great feeling to be together again.

He told me about his experience at the Ministry of Defense and how he had to nearly fight his way into the helicopter. After regaining our composure, we went up to the Air France ticketing agent and asked about our plane. We were told there would be a three-hour delay. Roy looked at me and in an assuring voice said,

"Don't worry, we'll stay here and wait no matter how long it takes."

I did not know how any plane could land under such weather conditions. Visibility was truly next to zero. Three hours later, in spite of the sandstorm, the Air France pilot landed the aircraft to our pleasant surprise. I looked at Roy laughingly and said,

"Only a nutty Frenchman would dare to attempt such a landing, but between you and me, I'm glad they're nuts."

The announcement came for all passengers to board when suddenly, a lady called to us from the back of the line. Why we were chosen from the multitude, I will never know; but there she was with four children standing around her. She asked if we would kindly look after these four kids as they were flying to New York without supervision. Of course, we asked her questions as to why no adult was accompanying them, and she explained, "These are my nephews and nieces. Their parents immigrated to the United States over a year ago, and the embassy didn't allow them to take their children along until they'd completed their paperwork in America. They've been staying with me all this time."

How cruel, I thought to myself. *Why would they separate families like this?* Without hesitation, we told her that we'd be glad to watch over them, so she tearfully kissed each child goodbye and thanked us for accepting. It was a humbling experience to see this kind of situation unfold.

We gathered the children along with ours and boarded together. As expected, the seating was different, and they were perhaps eight or nine rows behind us; so I got up several times during our trip to Paris to make sure they were doing well.

As the plane took off, Roy and I began to chuckle, thinking about that French pilot. He was either very courageous or very reckless, but both of us preferred to think that he was a courageously brilliant pilot. Approximately five hours later, Paris and Charles De Gaulle Airport welcomed us with bright lights and a clear evening sky.

Due to the delay, we missed our flight to New York, so a ground hostess made reservations for those in transit to stay that night at a motel near the airport with instructions to return the next morning at nine to our assigned gates. We all left on the shuttle that was waiting for us, assuming that everything was in order for our next day's flight.

After checking into our rooms, we took the children down to eat. I soon discovered that their parents did not know they were coming, so I asked the oldest of the four to give me their telephone number in New York. I needed to inform their family of the time we were landing. I also planned to call Roy's sister and her husband concerning the delay since they were coming to meet us, and theirs was a long trip from Connecticut to New York.

As I put the call through, a woman answered. She happened to be the sister of their father. I introduced myself and gave her the good news that the children were with us, asking that the parents meet us at Kennedy Airport the next day at the designated arrival time. To my surprise, she replied, "Sorry, I cannot believe you until I speak to the children. Please let me speak to them."

Puzzled by her response, I explained that they were still in the restaurant, eating; and as soon as they came up, I would put them through to her. I asked her why she was in such doubt about their coming, and she responded by saying, "We've received so many hoax telephone calls about the children arriving that we can no longer believe anything." I told her how sorry I was about the cruel mischief they had to endure and assured her this time they would have a pleasant surprise.

A half hour later, the children came up, and I called once again, giving the phone to the oldest child. I could tell there were tears of joy on both sides of the wide ocean that still separated them. When they finished, I took the receiver and asked her if she felt better. Of course, she replied, "Yes." She thanked me and apologized for her fears.

I was also able to reach Roy's sister, and now everything seemed in order, or so I thought. I accompanied the children to their room as it was time for all of us to retire after a grueling day.

The next morning after breakfast, the shuttle came and took us back to the airport. We arrived on time according to their instructions, but to our dismay, the ground hostess at the reservation desk looked at us and said, "Sorry, but your names are not on this flight, and you will have to be booked on a later one."

Only on rare occasions has Roy ever raised his voice, and this was one of them. He was very impressive and quite commanding. "What are you talking about?" he said. "Your people told us we were booked on this flight and to come in at this time. You don't omit names by mistake and expect people to pay for it. Now you turn yourself around and get us booked on that plane—*now!*"

She looked at him with eyes wide open, turned around, and began talking to some airline official at the door of the boarding area. Coming back, looking like a little mouse, she said, "Please excuse us, Colonel, but we have made a place for you and your two children. You may board."

Of course, Roy glared at her again and said, "What about the four children?" Her soft reply was, "Sorry, there is no room for them, they will have to leave tomorrow." Now Roy was ready to blow his top. After explaining our relationship to the children, he retorted, "Lady, we are not leaving without them. Get yourself back to those men over there and be sure to come back here with four other seats for those little kids."

Once again, she turned herself around, talked to the officials, and came back. "Colonel, we are giving your places to the children, and sorry, but we will have to put you and your family . . . in first class."

Sorry? *Wow*, what a turn of events. The good deed had produced its unanticipated reward.

After boarding, we were directed to the first-class section that had the most plush reclining seats I had ever seen while the area appeared more like a cathedral ceiling bedroom. A spiraling staircase, also nearby, took you to the captain's cabin.

Shortly after takeoff, they began to serve us meals from the famous Parisian restaurant, Maxim's. They never stopped feeding us throughout the entire trip. I recall our lunch consisted of the best French wine with an entrée of roast duck followed by the main course of roast beef with all the trimmings then fruit and desert. Trays of food were coming and going, and by the time we reached New York, I thought I had gained at least three pounds. The stewardess asked me later on, "Can I serve you anything else?" I replied, "Yes, ma'am, would you please get me some Tums for the tummy?" She smiled, but I was serious.

Approximately eight hours later, a welcoming committee at Kennedy Airport was there to meet us. It consisted of the children's parents and Roy's sister and brother-in-law. Four of the happiest kids were running toward their mom and dad, yelling and laughing as they grabbed hold of them; and for the first time, seeing their brand-new baby brother. It was a sight to behold. Through tears of joy, their parents graciously thanked us for accompanying their children. After we spoke for a while, each family left for a different destination. We still had another three-hour drive to Connecticut.

We spent two weeks with Roy's sister, and then put a call through to Dr. Brown in Texas. His wife, Shirley, answered the phone. She was elated to hear my voice as she did not know we were coming to the States. We spoke a while and then Shirley passed the phone to Dr. Brown who greeted me in his familiar Texas drawl.

"Hey, Noor. How y'all doing! Good to hear your voice. I want y'all to come down here. I need a teacher in the Christian elementary school I just opened for the first and second grade, and I've got an empty missionary apartment y'all can use for as long as you need till you get yourselves settled."

These words were like manna from heaven. I would not have to worry about a job while we were here. Of course, I accepted Dr. Brown's right-on-time offer.

Preparation for the trip was next on our agenda. I asked Roy's sister and her husband, George, if they could take us to some used-car dealership as we needed to find a vehicle we could afford. With only one thousand dollars in our pocket, we could not buy a car for more than six hundred. The remainder was for food, gas, and shelter; so we purchased the first car that fit our budget—a Chevrolet sedan. However, it was an older model four-speed car without any air conditioning, so we convinced ourselves that we were accustomed to the heat and to changing gears. Besides, it seemed to run fairly well.

I decided to place one more call to a dear couple, Dr. Metry and his wife, Margaret, who were living in Coral Gables, Florida. They were one of my parents' closest friends from the days of my childhood, and she was the lady who gave me the beaver coat years before. After I graduated from college in 1960, they invited me to come and stay with them for two weeks. At that time, Dr. Metry was the chief psychiatrist of the Florida State Mental Hospital in Fort Myers. They lived in a house within the confines of the hospital, and I must admit that it was one of the most interesting and enlightening experiences I'd ever had. In fact, I never forgot a comment that Dr. Metry made to me during one of our many conversations.

"Noor, I didn't see any real improvement in my patients until I was able to first plant the fear of God in their hearts, especially those who were on drugs, alcohol, or in depression."

Now that was one of the most surprising, yet profound, statements I'd heard coming from the lips of a scientist.

A Breath of Fresh Air

Seventeen years later, I was placing a call to Dr. Metry who was now retired. He could not believe that we were able to get out of Lebanon since the Beirut Airport had closed. They were delighted to know we were safe and invited us to come down and visit them. We called just in time since they were planning to leave three weeks later to his hometown, Charleston, West Virginia, for the remainder of the summer. This was their yearly exodus out of Coral Gables during the hot humid months. Now the plans for our trip to Dallas consisted of a detour to Florida, a few days at Disney World with the children, and then on to visit the Metrys.

Shortly after leaving Orlando, we started to experience problems with our car. It would suddenly choke and then stop. Each time the car jerked, I would ask God to help us get to our destination without having to stop at some strange repair shop. I had heard enough stories of people being ripped off by garage mechanics they did not know.

This problem began to seriously manifest itself about two hours before we reached Coral Gables. It kept on getting worse; and as we entered the city limits, our car came to a full stop.

Roy called Dr. Metry who immediately came with his mechanic and a tow truck. We left the car at the garage and returned the next day to the repair shop for the news. The mechanic discovered that the fuel pump was full of moisture, so he dismantled the gas tank only to find a third of it filled with water. Apparently, some very honorable people at a gas station had been spiking one of the gasoline reservoirs with water, and who would ever know since Route 95 was mostly a highway for tourists who were just passing through. The mechanic emptied the gas tank, made sure it dried, and then reinstalled it. It took two days to complete the job. In the meantime, we had a wonderful two-week visit before leaving for Texas.

Dr Metry had an indoor swimming pool just beyond the kitchen and sitting room area of his home. I remember one of his first comments at breakfast.

"Since we've been here, I've never invited any guests to come who have small children because I don't want to worry about their safety around the swimming pool." He paused a bit while cooking the bacon, and then continued. "You're the first people I've ever allowed to be here with kids. But we just had to see you, so please keep an eye on them."

Four days later, as you might have guessed, we were sitting near the pool while Margaret was grilling some rib-eye steaks for supper. Suddenly we heard a splash, and lo and behold, my three-year-old was in the water. I pulled her out in a matter of seconds, looked at Dr. Metry, and with doleful eyes and a smile to match, said, "Sorry, Doc, there's always a first time." There were no more accidents, and the remainder of our visit was very peaceful and pleasant.

We soon were on our way to Dallas, a trip that was long and tedious. Without any air-conditioning in the car, we sadly discovered just how hot Texas really was. The children, quite naturally, became cranky in the heat. However, the car did not give us any more trouble. The only problem we encountered was after entering the Dallas city limits. The numerous highways in front of us appeared very intimidating and confusing, so Roy decided not to follow my directions, thinking I was wrong about what exit we should take, and so we passed it by. Men can be stubborn when they think they know best. Of course, I was right and he was wrong, so we kept going in circles for more than an hour until we were back on track.

When we arrived at the church, Dr. Brown was still conducting the evening service, so we sat in a pew at the back of the sanctuary. Poor little Sandy was so tired that she fell asleep in my arms and began to snore. It was loud enough to attract the attention of people in the front pews. I could tell they preferred listening to a loud sermon instead of loud snoring, but there was very little I could do. It would not be until we returned to Lebanon a year later that we had her adenoids surgically removed, and thankfully, the snoring disappeared.

Now when the service was over, Dr. and Mrs. Brown quickly came to welcome us. After we visited for a short time with them, they accompanied us to the missionary apartment that became our home for the next several months.

That same evening, while getting ready for bed, we were also welcomed by a tornado that hit Dallas. We could see the funnel-shaped whirlwind from our window. The next day we learned that it actually blew the rooftops off many of the houses that surrounded the church and our apartment. Thankfully, it never came near the church premises. However, the thunder actually sounded louder to our ears than the bombs we left behind in Beirut. I could not help but find it a bit humorous that perhaps God wanted to make us feel right at home. As the tornado continued to rage, I smiled and said to Roy, "Do you know, I believe God is going to make sure we stay humble. I don't think he wants us to get used to having too much peace and quiet." Nevertheless, we all were still too tired from the trip to be worried about the winds and went to sleep in the midst of the storm.

The remainder of our time in the States was spent in Dallas where I taught both first—and second-grade students. We also had the opportunity to make new friends and minister to several young people who had recently become church members.

Two weeks after our arrival, Dr. Brown introduced us to a young married couple, Yvonne and Naim, who had come all the way from Amman, Jordan for ministry training at the church. They both took great comfort in us since we were the only people they met in Dallas who came from their part of the world and who spoke Arabic. Yvonne felt a little less homesick when she was around us.

There were also two young men whom we often invited to our home for a meal. They so appreciated the fact that we made them feel like members of our own family. When it was time to leave Dallas, they both volunteered to take us to the airport the day we were to fly out to Connecticut on our way home. I can never forget their sad faces as they told us how much they would miss us. It seemed that no church family had paid this much attention to them before or made them feel so welcomed. Roy and I were extremely glad we had been given the opportunity to make a difference in their lives and to let them know how important they were to us and to God.

Five months after our arrival in Texas, however, Roy was able to find a job as a draftsman and renew his leave of absence once again. We then vacated the missionary apartment and rented a flat on our own for the remainder of the time.

When we were ready to leave Dallas, we gave our car to the church and flew into Connecticut to see Roy's sister again. It was now January, and Beirut International Airport finally reopened. We stayed with my sister-in-law for one more week and then flew into Lebanon out of New York City. God's grace had given us the opportunity to spend nine wonderful months away from missiles, bombs, and streaking bullets with friends we loved dearly, but now it was time to go home.

Chapter 12

The Faith to Keep On

God is our refuge and strength, a very present help in trouble.
—Psalm 46:1

God had planned every step of our journey to America, and it was delightful. We were able to recover our strength and peace of mind, but seeing Lebanon from the skies once again made our hearts rejoice even though the war was far from over. Our faith and patience would be tested many times over. However, with each test, Roy and I held on in hope to the provisions and promises of God over our lives.

During our absence, the Lord miraculously protected our home from squatters. It seemed that as we did God's work in Dallas, he was taking care of ours in Beirut. I learned, however, that the couple from church did not remain long in our apartment. It seemed that many of their family members from a nearby Christian Palestinian refugee camp had visited them a bit too often, and they were becoming unmanageable. The couple finally decided to leave and give the keys back to our pastor.

A few weeks later, Suzie, a neighbor and friend from church, contacted a relative of hers who needed a place to stay. He was a left-wing Armenian who apparently was not welcomed much on the other side of Beirut, so my friend got the keys and let him in. He did take care of our home for a while and rewarded himself with a few bottles of our wine and some arak, a colorless Lebanese drink distilled from white grapes and anisette. That was perfectly fine with us since we hardly ever drank wine or arak. However, he left two months before we returned, and God protected our home for the remainder of the time.

I found the house extremely dirty and disheveled even though my friend, Suzie, had graciously come with her maid who collected and threw out twelve huge bags of garbage. Thus, the arduous task of cleaning an abandoned home began.

We also had no more than six hours of electricity a day, making my job even harder. Roy helped me all he could; but one week after our arrival, he had to report back to duty while it took me three more weeks, every single day from dawn till dusk, to finally get our house in order.

A short time later, I was diagnosed with viral hepatitis and bedridden for more than three weeks as I battled the disease. It left me so weak that my doctor prescribed injections of high dose B12, B1, and B6, which I took consecutively for fourteen days. It did the trick. Before the two weeks were over, I was jumping around with more pep and energy than I had before getting ill. At the same time, one new political crisis after another would erupt.

The Palestinian militiamen had been launching attacks into Israel from the areas they controlled on our southern border. The Israelis responded with severity as usual, and Lebanese civilians paid the price.

The Faith to Keep On

I often thought about the history of this group of people, the Palestinians, who now had become a thorn in the flesh of Lebanon. As a teenager in Akron, I had met an elderly gentleman by the name of Iskandar Nihani. He had been a guest speaker at our church on two separate occasions during his fund-raising campaigns for the orphanage and school he directed in the Beqaa Valley of Lebanon. However, I soon learned from his speech that the school was originally founded in Palestine. Nevertheless, it would not be until ten years later when we visited him at his home in Lebanon that I would learn the details of his personal story while in Palestine during the Arab-Israeli War of 1948.

Iskandar was an impressive white-haired man in his late fifties; a brilliant speaker and master of the English language as well as Arabic, French, and German. He also was distantly related to my father, so my parents decided to invite him to our home for dinner one evening during his stay in Akron.

We learned that he had worked as a translator with British Intelligence in the deserts of Arabia during World War I, and even more exciting was the fact that he was a close friend of Sir Lawrence of Arabia, one of the most colorful military figures of that period. Iskandar described how Lawrence, along with his band of Arab irregulars, attacked Turkish strongholds and destroyed railways to support the British army as they made their thrust into Damascus. Iskandar's tales of Lawrence's exploits against the Turks were mesmerizing.

As a teenager, my curiosity concerning the Palestinians had not yet matured, so our conversation went in another direction. I did learn, however, that after the end of World War I, Iskandar became the headmaster of the Schneller orphanage founded by German missionaries in Palestine. Schneller would be his home until 1948. That year, Iskandar, along with the children, escaped the ravages of the Arab-Israeli War by returning to his birthplace in the Beqaa Valley where the institute was rebuilt on the outskirts of his hometown, Kherbet Kanafar.

In the summer of 1964, Roy, my parents, and I journeyed to the Beqaa Valley to pay him a visit at his home. During our time there, I asked Iskandar to tell us more about his experience in Palestine and what really happened to these people. He spoke about the Arab-Israeli conflict that began after Israel declared its statehood and how he was forced to flee.

"It was for the sake of the children that I abandoned the school building and dorms, using whatever means of transportation available, mostly walking, to get to the Lebanese border and to safety."

Ironically, he and the orphans would pass through a small village called Deir Yassin where he discovered, to his horror, that Israeli terrorists had attacked only hours before and massacred over 200 of its peaceful citizenry. Those who had successfully hidden themselves remained alive to tell the story. He also recounted his shock at seeing a pregnant woman with her belly slashed open and the unborn baby half out of its mother's womb. He explained that this was one of the tactics used to make the Palestinians abandon their homes and flee in fear for their lives. Once out of the country, they were never allowed to return as those who fled had their homes confiscated "This," he continued, "was, in my opinion, another form of psychological warfare as a large number of Palestinians believed this would be their fate if they didn't flee also." I could now relate to the pain of these people even though I hated what they were doing to Lebanon. Iskandar's detailed account of the atrocities that had occurred against the Palestinians corroborated the articles and books I read on the subject. One article in particular talked about villagers being forced out at gunpoint with killings to speed them on their way in the twin villages of al-Ramla and al-Lydd. I had received enough of a history lesson to understand the agony of a people purposely displaced and caught in the cross fire of the warring factions—the Arabs and the Israelis.

It was now 1977, and sporadic fighting was taking place everywhere in Beirut between militias as countless innocent lives were snuffed out by missiles, snipers, and car bombs.

In spite of it all, we went to church in Ras Beirut nearly every Sunday morning and evening. Meetings were rarely canceled unless things became extremely dangerous. There were still many Americans around who were hoping that it would all be over soon because they really did not want to leave. The American embassy would sometimes publish a statement, warning its citizens that they were staying at their own risk; but most of us were willing to take the chance. Eventually, many did leave the country for fear of being kidnapped if they happened to be in the wrong place at the wrong time.

In March 1978, the attacks developed into an all-out Israeli assault, and more civilians died. I recall the United Nations Interim Peace Keeping Forces being deployed into the south to lessen the tension, making the Israelis pull back later.

Prior to that invasion, Syria, in 1976, had sent its army into Lebanon; and during the two years that ensued, they were occupying more regions in Lebanon, including parts of Beirut. Fear had set into the hearts of the civilian population as more and more car bombs exploded, sometimes killing as many as a hundred people at a time. The Syrians also began firing their missiles into the areas where they were not welcomed.

Many of the statesmen and journalists of Lebanon, who publicly denounced this foreign presence, were assassinated, and nobody dared point an accusing finger at anyone. Sadly, both of our neighbors, north and south, practiced assassinations. What might have appeared evident as to the identity of the culprit remained hidden in the reality of the foreign intrigue that pervaded Lebanon.

I remember one of the early examples of a journalist's assassination. This was a man by the name of Salim Al-Lawzi. He was a staunch opponent of Syrian occupation in Lebanon and wrote powerful articles on the subject without any compromise. Eventually he went into self-exile as his life had been threatened. Thinking he could go unnoticed, he made the fatal mistake of coming into Beirut International Airport several months later to attend his mother's funeral. He never made it and was later found dead. Gruesome photos showed the flesh of his right forearm and hand that he penned his articles with completely burned by acid while only the bones remained. The chilling pictures flashed in all the newspapers of Lebanon, giving the reader a grim foreboding of things to come.

The years passed, and there seemed to be no end to the belligerence. In 1979, I started teaching part-time at the Lebanese American University in Ras Beirut (formerly BUC) located approximately two miles away from our home as well as the Lebanese University situated in Al Fanar, a mountain village above East Beirut. Of course, I had to cross the green line to get there, which was quite an adventure if not downright dangerous. However I did schedule my classes in the morning on Tuesdays and Thursdays so that I crossed over only twice a week. That seemed to be the safest plan. The other days, I spent at LAU teaching two other courses. I continued on this schedule for the next three years.

One of my most incredible experiences occurred April 2, 1982. I could never forget the date because it happened to be my birthday as well. I left the house around 7:30 AM to go up and teach at the Lebanese University on the east side. My class started at nine, and all my students were present. By 9:30, we began to hear the bombing of the Christian areas by Syrian forces. It kept getting stronger and louder until the students were finally given permission by the administration to go home. As one of the missiles landed on the school grounds at approximately 10:15, my students panicked and began to run out of the building. I had to let them go although I felt it was unwise at the time. Later on, I learned that they all made it safely home. However, I could not leave at the same time they did since I had to make the very dangerous crossing into West Beirut.

The building was now practically empty, and the only company I had was a young Lebanese soldier who happened to be on sick leave. His leg had been severely injured from shrapnel while on duty, and he was still on crutches. He had come to pick up his niece, who was a student, but she had left with friends, and he too was stranded. Sitting in one of the administrative offices, we both decided to wait it out until the shelling subsided.

Roy was at his station near the green line crossing, and the children were at home alone. I knew they would be terribly worried if I did not show up as usual before noon. Cici had baked her very first cake to celebrate my birthday and was waiting for me to arrive.

My fear was that if I could not contact any of them, Roy would try to come up himself to get me, and I did not want this to happen.

I picked up the phone, but the line was dead. There was no sound whatsoever; and for at least an hour, I continued to pick it up, hoping that by some miracle I would hear the buzz of a dial tone. It appeared hopeless. Suddenly, a young man came rushing in with a belligerent look in his eyes and picked up the receiver to make a call. When he discovered the line was dead, he lifted the phone over his head with the intent of dashing it to pieces on the floor. He happened to be a member of a militia, and they were never too friendly or patient. Somehow, I mustered up the courage and raised my voice at him and said, "Stop what you're doing right now and put that phone back. Do you think that if you broke it, the line would return?"

When I got his attention, I repeated, but in a slightly softer tone, "Put it down, son, put it down."

Thank God, he did just that; and without saying a word, he turned around and left. Breathing a sigh of relief, I took the phone in my hand, got on my knees in front of the desk, and in utter desperation, I began talking to God. Knowing the very air that surrounded me was filled with his presence, I said, "Lord, you understand my need right now. I must put a call through, so I ask you to please send your angel to give me, just this one time, a phone line so I can talk to my family to let them know I'm safe; and if you do, Lord, please tell me who to call."

I just continued my conversation with God and said, "I know there must lines out there that are just as dead as this one, so please give me the wisdom to make the right choice. Do I call home or Roy's office? Thank you, Lord. Amen."

Still kneeling, I laid my hand on the receiver; and as I picked it up, a dial tone—loud and clear as a bell—came through. What a miracle! My God had answered my prayer. From a still small voice, I could hear the words, "Call home."

I immediately dialed our house number, and in less than three rings, Cici answered. What an awesome Master we serve. There were no words to describe the joy and peace I felt, being able to talk to my little girls and giving them the instructions they needed as well as putting their minds at ease.

I explained to Cici she would have to be the one to call her father at work. Her instructions were to tell him not to worry, that I would remain at the university until I felt it was safe to leave, and not try to come after me.

The soldier was now waiting his turn to call, but after I finished telling Cici what to do, I turned to the soldier and said, "I know this is the only line we'll get; so give me a number you'd need to contact, and I'll have my daughter make the call for you."

He was so grateful and graciously gave me the number of a place where he thought his wife would be at that time. I thanked God again for the miracle and closed the phone. This time when I picked it up, it was completely dead. I asked for one call that day and received it. We would hear no more dial tone afterward.

Waiting was difficult, but we stuck it out; and by one o'clock, the shelling became less frequent. We then decided it was time to take a chance and head for home. We each started our descent toward the coast. I was driving the same 1963 Ford Zodiac Roy had purchased when we first got married. It was nearly twenty years old, and the steering wheel somehow got out of alignment weeks before and would constantly wiggle and rock back and forth between my hands. It was quite funny to see me drive that car, especially on the turns. The mechanic who checked it said it was not a dangerous problem. We trusted his judgment as the opportunity to repair whatever was broken never presented itself. Now I would be driving under very precarious conditions, so to keep my mind off the wriggling steering wheel, I began to sing a hymn in Arabic entitled "If God Be for Us, Who Can Be Against Us." I could not think of a more appropriate hymn. Thankfully, my steering wheel remained intact. In fact, we never did repair it.

Reaching the bottom of the mountain, we waved good-bye at each other and parted company as the soldier turned right to go home, and I turned left toward Beirut.

There were absolutely no cars on the road, and everywhere I looked, all I could see was a misty haze that appeared to control the atmosphere around me. I felt chills going up and down my spine for a few seconds.

I began to muster up my courage as a new dilemma was facing me. I looked up and began talking to my Father in heaven once again.

"Lord, I want to pass by Roy on my way home, and you know there are many roads that go in that direction. Please show me which one is safe to take, Amen."

As soon as I had finished, I caught sight of a lonely military jeep on the coastal highway perhaps a hundred yards away from me, traveling in the direction I needed to take, and I said, "Thank you, Lord! You just sent an angel to guide me."

I simply followed the vehicle, and in fifteen minutes, I was close enough to Roy's office building so that I could part company with the jeep. I made a left turn off the highway on to a narrow street that was familiar to me. Once again, the road was empty.

Less than five minutes away from my destination, I began to hear sounds that I first thought were an array of bullets being fired somewhere in the distance. A short while later, a car filled with a

The Faith to Keep On

group of teenage boys came speeding toward me from the opposite direction. The young driver looked back as he passed me by and yelled, "Hey, lady, you've got a real bad flat tire in the rear." My first fleshly thought was, "Oh, Lord, how could you bring me this far to let this happen?"

I'm sure God was laughing at me for having questioned his wisdom and mercy as I got out of the car to check my little catastrophe. He had already done so much for me, and now I was questioning whether he was going to finish the job. I looked at my left rear tire, and sure enough, it had torn to shreds. I was driving on the rim, and the sound I was hearing was actually the tire ripping apart. I put my hands on my waist wondering what to do next.

Suddenly, I saw a young man come out of nowhere, walking toward me. He said very politely, "Can I help you, ma'am?" "Oh, absolutely," I replied. His kind response was, "I will be glad to, but I've never changed a tire before. Just tell me what to do." I thought it strange that a young man his age did not know how to change a tire; nevertheless, I gladly gave him instructions. I opened the trunk and asked him to take out the spare tire with all the tools. He got started, and in just several minutes, the job was done.

The young gentleman stood behind me as I placed the jack and tools back into the trunk. When I turned around to thank him, he was nowhere in sight. Deep in my heart, I knew this had to be a real encounter with an angel sent by God to help me. I believe my mother had said enough prayers of protection over my head as a child that God placed into an account he could draw from for the rest of my life. Surely, this had to be one of those times.

I finally arrived at the building where Roy's sixth-floor office was located. He and his friends were out on the balcony, apparently waiting for me because as I drove toward the curb, they all began to wave wildly as if they had witnessed my resurrection. It certainly was a very happy reunion, and I was able to tell them the whole story while they listened intently.

The shelling had intensified once again, so I waited an additional two hours that afternoon before we decided I should try to head out. In the meantime, I was able to call the children from Roy's office. Happy to hear my voice, they were anxiously waiting for me to get home. After all, this was my birthday, and the cake was ready for the celebration.

The times were so chaotic that even Roy did not know which road would be the safest for me to take. There were several possibilities, but which one to choose was a puzzle. This had been an incredible day, having one supernatural encounter after another with an awesome God. He had answered my prayers and sent me an angel, but it was not over yet.

Roy and some of his officer friends accompanied me down to the street; and as we all walked to the curb, a car suddenly drove by with two of my friends from church, who lived approximately one mile away. They were coming from my side of Beirut; and as they stopped to greet us, without my asking, they said, "Hi, Noor, we just crossed over from West Beirut, and the best road to take is the one that goes to the airport. Then you can connect to the Corniche, and you'll be on your way home."

The puzzle was solved. Had I delayed coming down just a minute longer, I would have missed them, but God had other plans and made me move right on time. Roy sent one of his soldiers who needed a ride home to accompany me. He and his family did not live too far from our apartment, so it was convenient for him as well as for me.

We were still passing through roads where there were militia checkpoints, but they were not belligerent, and the soldier tried to look as much like a civilian as possible. No one stopped us as we drove through. I dropped him off near his house and continued on my way.

I arrived home a few minutes later to see my children waiting on the balcony and cheering me on. It was quite a family reunion, and Cici could hardly wait to show me the birthday cake. It was the first one she had ever baked, and when the time came to place a candle in the center, it just would not penetrate the surface. I could tell that if you threw the cake on the wall, it would bounce back. We all laughed and hammered out three portions; one for each of us to eat. I did not care how hard it was. After all, my daughter had made it, and that was what counted—just as long as I did not break a tooth.

Chapter 13

The Pressure Mounts

Yea, though I walk through the valley of the shadow of death, I will fear no evil: for Thou art with me.
—Psalm 23:4

It was now becoming more dangerous to cross to the east side, so I decided to resign from my position at the Lebanese University. The school tried to wind up its affairs as quickly as possible; thus, we terminated the school year—which normally ended in May—six weeks early and gave the final exams as well.

To make matters worse, I was diagnosed with breast cancer. I had gone in for my yearly visit to the gynecologist, but when the doctor pronounced the C-word, I felt as if the rug had suddenly been pulled out from under me. I found myself once again in one of my low times as I tried to clear my very confused mind. It was as if the doctor had pronounced a death sentence, and once again I began to think of what would happen to Roy and the children if something happened to me.

I left his clinic and walked slowly down the street to my car. Completely oblivious to those around me, tears began to flow down my cheeks. At home, I broke the news to Roy, and he started to cry

The Pressure Mounts

with me; and oh, how I hate seeing men cry! It tore me up even more as dark thoughts began to run through my mind.

A few days later, I made an appointment to see a general surgeon who immediately sent me to the lab for a needle biopsy. The results came out positive. That was the clincher; and being a surgeon, he encouraged us to have the operation performed as soon as possible.

By this time, Roy and I had joined another Baptist church; and that same evening, we were having a guest evangelist, a truly gifted speaker, for a series of revival meetings. He was Lebanese and founder of that particular church many years back, but he and his family had been living in the United States for a number of years. It was an awesome evening, but I was still feeling miserable.

At the conclusion of the service, we met the evangelist, Yousef Costa, outside. He looked at me and said, "Noor, why do you look so depressed? Tell me what's wrong."

Of course, I shared with him the news and all my fears. Full of compassion, he addressed my anxiety.

"I was diagnosed with cancer several years ago too, but I'm well now, and you'll be well also. I know it. God is always in control and he is the Healer. You must believe that!"

"My faith has been tried too many times, Pastor," I replied. "And even though I don't feel it, I'll trust the One who pulled me through."

I was once again in the crucible of testing. He prayed over me and then gave me a beautiful verse out of the Bible that kept him uplifted throughout his ordeal.

"Open your Bible and turn to Isaiah 3:10 and read it,"

As I did, a surge of peace and joy I had not felt since my diagnosis came over me. The verse read, *Say ye to the righteous that it shall be well with him.* Those words were to be my companion from that moment on.

It did not take Roy and me too long to decide I would go in for surgery at the American University Hospital. My morale was now very good, and I had asked the elders of my church to have a special prayer meeting for me and to anoint me with oil just as the Bible directed in the Book of James 5:14-16, *Is any sick among you? Let him call for the elders of the church; and let them pray over him anointing him with oil in the name of the Lord: And the prayer of faith shall save the sick, and the Lord shall raise him up; and if he have committed sins, they shall be forgiven.*

We made an appointment to meet in the pastor's office that evening where I received prayer. There were four elders, my husband, and the pastor who anointed me with oil. I knew that God had answered my prayer in that room.

I was admitted to the hospital the day before the scheduled surgery. Morning came, and as they wheeled me into the operating room, the surgeon accompanied me down the long corridor. It gave me the opportunity to tell him of my concerns and exactly what I expected of him.

"Doctor, my mother was a victim in this very hospital because one particular surgeon allowed his interns to practice stitching her up, and she died. I want you to promise me that no other doctor or student will touch me when you begin to operate."

He turned to me with doleful eyes, and said, "I promise, Noor."

"One more thing, Doc. Are you planning on giving me any medications afterwards?"

"No, you won't be needing any, unless you have pain."

"I don't plan on having any pain, Doctor, but thank you anyway."

The Pressure Mounts

I had asked the right question because the next day, a nurse came in with a pill. I looked her straight in the eye and said, "Nurse, go back and call the doctor in. He hasn't prescribed any pills for me."

Certain that I was wrong, she found him outside my room as he just happened to be making his rounds on the floor. I could hear their conversation from my bed, and his rebuke was quite sharp and angry. Apparently, she had read somebody else's chart. He came into my room afterward and apologized for the mistake. I began to wonder how many people are given wrong medications during their stay in hospitals and how many die because of it. As far as I was concerned, just one was one too many.

I was told that the surgery had taken approximately three and a half hours. He had performed a radical mastectomy just to be safe. I later learned that studies had shown no increase in lifespan because of such a radical procedure, but it was too late now. In the recovery room, however, I began to wake up without feeling much discomfort and without any pain afterward.

The following morning, a nurse introduced me to a simple stretch exercise since I could no longer raise my arm any higher than a few inches. I simply placed the palm of my hand on a wall and with my fingers, moved my arm up as high as possible, and then back down as many times as I could. I practiced this routine faithfully every single hour until I could reach well above my head several days later.

While in the hospital, I enjoyed going from room to room on my floor, seeing if anybody needed prayer. Right next door to me was a precious Muslim lady named Miriam, who was having surgery on her leg for the seventh time. We immediately became friends as we each shared our story. The next morning, I went into her room and prayed with her before they wheeled her into the operating suite. Several hours later, as they rolled her out of the recovery room to her bed, the whole corridor of patients and visitors could hear her screams from the unbearable pain in spite of the drugs they had given her to ease her suffering.

During our first conversation, she told me of a major car accident she had in Saudi Arabia where her husband worked. A doctor at a Saudi hospital immediately placed her leg in a cast, which cascaded into a series of bone-splintering episodes. Miriam had gone through several surgeries to remove the splinters that kept recurring. As her problem became chronic, she flew back to her home in Beirut to be under the supervision of some of the very best bone specialists in the area. There was no need to imagine how painful and agonizing this problem had become, for I was a witness to her excruciating pain.

As her cries grew louder, I could not help but go to her side. Her mother, a very conservative Muslim lady with a tight scarf tied around her head, sat helplessly on a chair next to her. I do not know how I got the courage, but I boldly told her I was going to pray over her daughter in the name of Jesus, and hoped she would not have any problem with that. She was desperate and did not object at all. I really didn't know what God was going do, and I was shaking. I only knew God had to be glorified in all this, but would he answer my prayer quickly?

I laid my hands on Miriam who was fully awake and alert. I had already spoken to her about Jesus the day before, and she was very receptive to all that I had said about his love and his desire to heal her. She looked at me and cried out in agony, "Noor, please pray for me!"

I closed my eyes and began to pray out loud, asking Jesus to please heal her and take her pain away. It was not a long prayer, but there was faith behind it, more of hers than mine; and as soon as I had finished, I opened one eye and peeked. To my surprise, she had fallen asleep like a baby with a peaceful smile on her face.

Suddenly, I saw her mother rush toward me with eyes wide open and hands ready to grab hold, and all I could think of saying was, "Look, dear lady, that was not me. I had nothing to do with your daughter falling asleep. It was all the work of my Lord Jesus. Please sit down."

To my surprise, she did, with a grateful smile on her face and a thank-you on her lips. I replied, "Please thank Jesus, not me," and left the room. Miriam slept for the remainder of the day, and when she woke up that evening, there was no more pain.

When my pastor came to visit me, I told him what had happened, and asked him to buy me a leather-bound New Testament with the pages edged in gold. I wanted to give it to Miriam as a gift.

The following day, I entered her room with the Bible; and as I drew near her bed, she hugged me. I said to her,

"Miriam, this book tells the story of the one who healed you yesterday. Would you like to receive him as your Lord and Savior?" Her reply was a resounding *yes*.

We prayed the sinner's prayer together, and I gave her the New Testament with the following verse written for her in Arabic by my pastor. *For God so loved the world that he gave his only begotten Son that whosoever believed in him should not parish but have everlasting life.* (Jn 3:16)

She kissed the Bible, and as she placed it to her bosom, Miriam cried out in Arabic, "Ya habibi ya Yesua," which translated means *my beloved Jesus*. Tears came to my eyes as I said, "Do you know,

Miriam, we may never have an opportunity to see each other again outside this hospital, but I do know one thing; we'll be seeing each other one day in heaven. You and I have become sisters in Christ, and nothing can ever separate us from that."

Once again, she received that word with more joy than I had ever seen on anyone's face. I'm certain her life was never the same again. It is true that after my discharge from the hospital, I never saw her except for a brief moment when I was walking across the street near the hospital a few weeks later. She was on the other side, too far away for us to meet, but we did wave at each other for the last time.

Nineteen eighty-two was full of sad surprises. Less than two weeks after my surgery while I was still recuperating, Israel made its second invasion into Lebanon. The Lebanese military had gotten word of this impending assault, so Roy came home and told me to quickly pack a few things for the children and myself as he was taking us to his brother's house in the mountain area of Klayaat for safety. I was so angry that foreigners were invading my land and my privacy so that I would not be able to continue recuperating in the comfort of my own home. I now had to seek refuge for whatever time was necessary until some sort of order returned.

As we crossed the green line to the other side, Roy stopped at the home of one of our friends, Louis, who also was a male nurse at AUB hospital. We had been friends with him and his family for many years, and he kindly took care of all my needs at the hospital during my six-day stay after the surgery. His home where he resided with his wife and five children was very close to Roy's work. The offices of the Radar Division had been moved into the Lebanese Civil Defense building deeper into East Beirut and less than half a mile from Louis's house.

Our friend absolutely refused to take no for an answer when he invited us to stay with them for the duration of the crisis. He felt that Roy would be able to come and see the children and me more often if we were closer than in some distant mountain village.

He and his family were the epitome of Lebanese kindness and hospitality. Their house consisted of only one bedroom, and their children slept on sofa beds in the living and dining room areas. He and his wife had graciously given up their only bedroom for my family and me. The two beds were quite large; thus, my daughters were able to share one of them. Louis and his wife slept on the living room sofas while two of their children slept on floor mattresses. It was an incredible time, and miraculously, none of us felt any discomfort in the small living space.

A few days later, Israel began its invasion in an attempt to derail the Palestinian resistance by forcing their armed guerrillas out of Lebanon. But this time, they entered the very heart of Beirut, bombing Palestinian camps as well as civilian buildings that were not far from our own home on the west side. In fact, one eight-story building was razed to the ground with many of its inhabitants in it.

The Israelis had been training and equipping the Lebanese forces, (the Christian Phalangist militia) inside Israel, and they had learned their lessons well. This incursion apparently was planned with the blessings of the Israeli military over this militia that also wanted to be rid of the Palestinian presence in Lebanon. However, many Lebanese died as well. *Collateral damage* is the euphemism politicians as well as the press use when innocent civilians are killed, be they Palestinians or Lebanese.

In the Hands of the Refiner

Situated a short distance from Louis's home is the beautiful Beirut Forest, full of tall pine trees that were at least a hundred years old. If you ever flew over Beirut in the daytime, you could look out the porthole and see a bright green carpet woven by the branches of those very same trees. Strangely, the Israelis began an assault on that forest and the surrounding area; the excuse being a Palestinian presence. I personally never saw a single Palestinian hiding under the trees they saw fit to destroy.

When the Israelis launched their vicious air attack on Beirut, I counted each bomb run as the missiles came crashing. I heard more than 250 major air strikes in that one day that destroyed over 70 percent of the forest as well as many of the buildings that surrounded it. We could not even hear ourselves speak because the noise was so intense.

The day before the air strike, it was relatively quiet; so my friend, Suzie, who had taken care of our home back in 1976, came to visit us with her children. She, of course, knew Louis and his family very well; and at Louis's invitation, decided that it was safe enough to leave her two girls, Grace and Joyce, with us overnight as her daughters were close friends with mine. The next morning, however, things took a turn for the worse, and the air strikes began, making it impossible for Suzie to pick up her children.

Throughout the unceasing Israeli bomb runs, which lasted throughout the day, I gathered all the children into the living room and asked them to start singing the church hymns they knew in Arabic; and in between songs, we read most of the Book of Psalm. That day I was to discover the power of praise and worship that invited God's presence. None of the children displayed any fear, nor did any of them jump from the shock of the sound waves. I felt as if there were angels covering our ears so that no harm would befall any of us.

Sound waves can be extremely damaging to the brain and all related functions and organs. Soon after, Roy learned that the four-year-old son of his friend, Azad, began experiencing seizures shortly after that terrible day. Eventually, Azad took the child to America for medical treatment. Many of our neighbors also suffered migraine headaches, loss of hearing, or other neurological disorders from the horrific noise. The Israelis were actually flying so low that it sounded as if the planes were no more than a hundred feet above our heads. The days that followed were ugly, and the aftermath was the death of the innocent—as usual.

One month later, we were able to return to our apartment. Much had happened around us, but God in his infinite mercy protected our home and many others in the area as well. However, this would be a year of endless conflict and humiliation for many.

Israel was still in Lebanon and had planted its unwelcome presence in the South after destroying a number of villages. This began the twenty years of Israeli occupation on one side along with that of the Syrians on the other. *What a strange combination*, I thought. Lebanon as usual was in the cross fire of two enemies that never actually fired at each other—only at the Lebanese or Palestinians.

In direct violation of the ceasefire agreement that governed the PLO evacuation, Israeli forces moved into West Beirut on September 15, 1982. It was also a breach of promise made to President Ronald Reagan not to enter any part of West Beirut as plans for the exit of the PLO out of Lebanon were being implemented.

Prime Minister Menachem Begin and Israeli Defense Minister Ariel Sharon had made their own decision to go in with Sharon, observing over a period of three days one of the worst massacres ever perpetrated inside the Palestinian camps.

Whenever we had electricity, I followed the events on TV while Roy read the newspapers. Power cuts were still the order of the day, but what we heard and read disturbed us greatly.

Thursday, September 16, three units of the Phalangist militiamen were placed at the edge of Sabra and Shatila, two Palestinian refugee camps located in the heart of Beirut south of the green line about a mile away from the once beautiful Beirut Forest. These militiamen had unwittingly become proxies for Israel and were waiting for their orders from the Israeli military command headed by Ariel Sharon to go into the camps.

Although the Israelis did not enter themselves, they surrounded Sabra and Shatila with their tanks and soldiers so nobody could go in or out. By late afternoon, the Phalangist militiamen were given the orders to enter and then did not halt their murder spree until Saturday morning. The Israelis did nothing to hide their role in this insidious plan to massacre every man, woman, and child that lived inside the camps. I could never imagine anyone in his right mind committing such acts of barbarism—unless he had been given a hallucinatory drug like LSD. I later learned that many of these young men who decided to quit this particular militia had to be put in a drug rehab program by the Lebanese Army before they were able to function in society again.

Later on, we read the newspaper coverage of the results of an Israeli Commission of Inquiry into the facts of this massacre. According to the testimony given by Rafael Eitan, Israel's chief of staff, he admitted to working with Sharon on the whole scenario with the approval of the Israeli cabinet coming after the plan was activated. One of the generals who commanded the Israeli forces in Lebanon also admitted that Eitan met with the head of the Phalangist militia and congratulated him for doing such a good job.

No one will ever really know the exact number of casualties as many bodies were thrown into mass graves made by the parties who perpetrated this ungodly deed. However, the official head count rested at well over two thousand, a quarter of whom were poverty-stricken Lebanese, and the remainder, Palestinians. One can go into the archives of the *Washington Post* service of September 23, 1982, and read the gruesome description of the scene.

I recall that in December, the United Nations had enough evidence to declare the Sabra-Shatila massacre a genocide. However, nothing ever came of it. Sharon and his cohorts went free. In the kind of world we live in, it appears that only those who have no backing from the Western Powers, especially the USA, face international military tribunals for war crimes as did President Slobodan Miloševi for the massacres of Kosovo in 1999. I feel such shame that America sits back and says nothing when crimes against humanity are committed by Israel. There is a terrible double standard in operation on the American political stage that must be addressed.

During the same Israeli invasion of Beirut, I remember how their soldiers would go around, checking the downtown areas, especially where the jewelry shops were, looking at the windows in amazement as if they had never seen such things in their lives before. Many of our friends also observed them near their tanks completely nude, preparing to bathe under their makeshift showers for every passerby on the street to see. They were quite shameless in their display of *civility*.

After the Israelis withdrew from Beirut, we had to contend with the militiamen who were now at odds with each other.

By 1983, I started once again to teach a few courses at the Lebanese American University. It was then that Roy and I had the pleasure of meeting, for the first time, a young man from Austria by the name of Hannes. He had lived in Beirut for a number of years and remained even during the war in spite of the kidnapping of foreigners. A missionary and physiotherapist, he worked as a volunteer among the Palestinians in their camps and had built a wonderful relationship with them. The love and respect he showed these people broke the boundaries of ethnicity and religion.

However, in 1988, Hannes became a victim as well as an eyewitness to the attacks perpetrated this time by Islamic militiamen from the Shiite Amal movement against the Palestinians. He happened to be working in the camps the day the militia began a siege which lasted for six months, preventing food and other supplies from getting in or anyone from getting out.

Hannes's own gripping tale of survival never made headlines, but we were among the few to ever hear the story from his own lips: It seemed that he and one female nurse were the only foreigners working inside the camp on that fateful day. Certainly no one was prepared for such a terrifying event; and without any hope of escape, people began to panic. As the days turned into weeks and the weeks into months, every bit of food was finally gone. Sadly, the camp was a concrete jungle without any gardens or fruit trees to depend on; and now they and the Palestinians who refused to give up, began to eat cats, dogs, rats and anything that crawled to survive. Thankfully, Hannes along with the nurse made it through; but many Palestinians, especially the elderly as well as children, died of starvation before it was over.

The Palestinians became our neighbors whether we liked it or not, but they were not treated as neighbors—not by the Israelis, not by the Lebanese, not by anyone.

The Pressure Mounts

These people endured much as the world turned its back on them in indifference. They certainly were not *happy campers*. Unfortunately, prejudice and discrimination, like a double stick of dynamite with a short fuse, explodes quickly when lit and destroys everything in its path. Because of this, the Palestinians, (who also learned to practice the dark art of discrimination) have paid a terrible price along with the people who have refused to be their neighbors. We may ask ourselves, *what is the solution to this dilemma?* The answer is in the Bible.

In Luke 10:26, a lawyer was trying to tempt Jesus by asking, *Master, what shall I do to inherit eternal life?* Jesus replied, *What is written in the law? How readest thou?* The lawyer answered, **Thou shalt love** *the Lord thy God with all thy heart, and with all thy soul, and with all thy strength and with all thy mind; and* **thy neighbor as thyself**. (Emphases mine)

Jesus's response was the clincher as he said, *Thou hast answered right: this do,* **and thou shalt live**. (Emphasis mine)

In spite of the years of turmoil, I had many interesting experiences as an instructor at LAU. I taught some wonderful college students who went on to do great things in their chosen professions while others with a big chip on their shoulders sadly remained members of one militia group or another.

I recall one young Muslim student by the name of Monsour who would often get into fights in the university cafeteria. He had enough quilt-shaped scars from knife wounds on his belly to make one. Being a member of a Shiite militia, he often had misunderstandings with other students who were from opposing groups. However, he always showed me a great deal of respect and appreciation as his instructor.

One day I felt led to take him aside and share Jesus with this angry young man. When I did, he became very emotional. Welcoming all that I had to say, he listened intently and thanked me for caring. I never knew what happened to him after that. I could only pray that a seed had been planted into his life that would lead him away from violence into a relationship with the author of life, Jesus Christ, to whom he had been introduced on that particular day

Chapter 14

A Time to Reflect, a Time to Decide

Why do the heathen rage, and the people imagine a vain thing? . . . the rulers take counsel together against the Lord and against His anointed.
—**Psalm 2:1, 2**

In 1983, I witnessed with great disappointment the United States shirk its responsibilities toward Lebanon and toward itself.

The marines had landed, and the hope of a new beginning among many of the citizenry ran high. After all, America was a great Christian nation with moral values they hoped to count on. Many Lebanese told me they truly believed the United States would save the day by ridding Lebanon of foreign occupation and the militants as well.

The marines had set up their headquarters in a building near the Beirut Airport. They simply maintained a presence, which included guarding their premises. Somehow, their guard was down the day a truck loaded with heavy explosives entered the compound without being checked or even stopped. The minute the truck was inside, the driver carried out the insidious suicide mission. Over two hundred of America's finest soldiers were killed in an instant. Instead of responding, our government took it and ran. Once again, the Lebanese, and unknowingly the American people as well, had been let down by the great giant.

I believe that 9/11 became another infamous day in the history of our great nation as nearly three thousand souls paid the ultimate price because the threat of terrorism was not properly addressed many years back.

America possesses the strongest double-edged sword the world has ever known—its military might, and its moral diplomacy—but it used neither at the appropriate time. As a consequence, our embassies in several countries were destroyed, and many lives were lost. Ironically, when our embassy in Beirut was bombed, many more Lebanese staff members and visitors were killed than Americans. My friend, Renee, who had stayed with me for three weeks during the civil war, worked as a telephone operator at the embassy; and God in his mercy protected her from being one of the victims.

Sadly, terrorists targeted the Twin Towers the first time, and no one responded. The attack on the USS *Cole* claimed the lives of seventeen of our sailors, and we still did not move. Then came 9/11, and the president finally took action. All America rallied behind him as people started to go back to church. It appeared as if we were on the road to regaining our stature and moral compass. But alas, just a short time later, the petty games politicians play began, and the church pews became empty once more.

Our country entered Afghanistan and set the captives free from the terror of the Taliban. We entered a just war in Iraq, and as churches prayed, it appeared that we were winning. Then petty politicians came on the scene again; we stopped praying, and our country began to experience setbacks while becoming a divided nation, still looking to Wall Street (a house built on sand) as the barometer to our success.

With so many political failures behind us, I have learned never to lean for support on the arm of flesh. That is why we are commanded to intercede in prayer for our leaders. For even if they be virtuous men, they still need wisdom to make right decisions. Prayer can turn things around when we realize that *the heart of the king is in the hands of the Lord"* (Prv 21:1)

As I reflect on this new invasion of Lebanon, I cannot understand how a nation created out of the ghettos and concentration camps of Europe could become so cold, so callous, so indifferent to the cries of children being killed from the air. I will never understand how those whose families had been exterminated in the gas chambers and death camps of Hitler had now become exterminators from the sky. The Old Testament gave them permission to take out "an eye for an eye and a tooth for a tooth," but they were taking out a hundred eyes for each eye and a hundred teeth for each tooth. They simply had become a heartless war machine, excusing themselves before a world that no longer could discern right from wrong. Our politicians, the media, and many church leaders applauded and justified their actions as a war on terror.

Many in the TV audiences of America were thrust into the role of accessories after the fact, watching and waiting, doing nothing. They could now enter the theater of their own living rooms and see the gory movie unfold before their eyes, a soap opera the media was creating with their melodramatic assessment of the situation. That twenty—or fifty-inch tube was becoming the mother, the father, the teacher, the babysitter to all who would stare rather than watch because watching meant you were standing guard and taking action.

World conscience was being choked; the ability to make moral decisions atrophied as we were turned daily into robots whose job was to *turn it on* or *turn it off* at whim.

Honey, get me a bottle of beer and make some popcorn. I wanna watch the Israelis kill those sons of a b—before the basketball game starts.

I can imagine others saying, *Oh my God, those poor people.* Then they turn it off and go to bed. News that was meant to inform and stir its audience into taking a moral stand on issues had disappeared while it became entertainment on demand. The *Brave New World* of Huxley was taking shape before our eyes.

I cannot understand how my brothers in Christ—especially the self-appointed prophets of God, the televangelists—can boast with joy that this was the sign of the coming apocalypse. While the people in Lebanon were dying each day by the hundreds, they applauded and prayed only for the victory and safety of Israel. They seem to have forgotten that according to the New Testament, we are living in a period of grace so spectacular that God's love engulfs the whole world, not just a segment called the chosen people. They forgot the most quoted verse of all, and one that I had written long ago on the front page of Miriam's Bible.

For God so loved the world that He gave His only begotten Son… (Jn 3:16)

They forgot that there are people groups in the Arab world and the Middle East who need to hear the good news of the gospel instead of listening to the religious pundits rejoice in their demise, perhaps closing the door to any hope of salvation.

In all my years of attending church in America, I never heard a single prayer go up for the people of Palestine, Iraq, Iran, or Lebanon for that matter—or any other group in that region that needed Christ—until the recent Iraqi War. It was a done deal. Let them go to hell. Prayer was, and still is, focused on Israel alone. Of course, the Israelis need Christ; and certainly, we should pray for them. But prayer should be for their salvation, not just for the protection of a state at the expense of another in order that prophesy might be fulfilled.

Until now, Israel has never depended on God for its protection. They have the mightiest military machine in the whole of the Middle East put together backed by the money and might of the greatest power on earth today, the United States of America. Where does God fit into this equation?

"Come and let us reason together", just as the Lord asks us to do with him. Perhaps we will get more insight as to how God operates in protecting the nation of Israel in times of battle.

In the book of Joshua, chapter 6, God directs him (Joshua) to compass the city of Jericho with his men of war and seven priests, bearing before the Ark of the Covenant seven rams' horns. He commands them to walk around the mighty fortress once each day for six days. On the seventh day, the priests were to blow the trumpets at a specific time after they had all walked around Jericho seven times. Then all the people were to give a mighty shout. I'm sure what they did appeared quite humorous to the people inside the walls. No weapons of warfare were used, and guess what! The Israelites had obeyed every command of God. And when that final shout entered the atmosphere, the walls came tumbling down, and the enemy was defeated.

In the book of Judges 7:7, we find God commissioning Gideon to fight against the mighty army of the Midianites, using only three hundred men to do it instead of the twenty thousand that had gathered, and Israel was given the victory.

In the Hands of the Refiner

In 1 Samuel 17, when the Almighty had David confront Goliath, he equipped him with only five smooth stones to bring the giant down.

In the book of 2 Kings 19, we see King Hezekiah and Jerusalem confronted by the most ruthless army of that day, the Assyrians, under the leadership of King Sennacherib. That night, the Lord commands the Israelites to do nothing as he dispatches his warring angels from heaven to smite the enemy. By early morning, Hezekiah and all of Jerusalem wake up to see their victory accomplished at the hands of God.

Although there are many such stories in the Old Testament, let us go for one more from the New Testament and see how God operates.

In the fullness of time, he sends his only begotten Son, Jesus Christ, into the world. In order to establish his kingdom, Jesus must do warfare. Only now, the orders have changed. He comes and turns the world upside down, destroying the power of the enemy, Satan, with only one banner and one weapon in his arsenal—his obedience and his love!

Do you not see that when God is at work for a nation, he uses the least and does the most or he can never get the glory? He says to us, "Cursed is the man who leans on the arm of flesh." Israel has leaned on America for its salvation. It has depended on the cluster bombs, the mines, and whatever horrific weapons of warfare it wanted. My prayer is that Israel will get its priorities in order.

I read scripture after scripture to be sure I understood God's will in all that was happening, and he did reveal it to me; for I was searching in the spirit of truth, not trying to find evidence to support some lopsided political point of view. It was not anything like the conclusion many televangelists had pronounced to the world and to brainwashed congregations when they demanded the blind uncompromising support for the state of Israel. Such a mindset in Old Testament times would have nullified all the warnings of the ancient prophets when they told Israel to turn from their wicked ways so that the blessings of God would come upon them. Without recognizing it, they were becoming the voices of Balaam.

Many other pastors even claimed that the Jewish people did not need Jesus since they already obtained salvation by the old covenant. In reality, they too have taken on the role of Balaam, doing just as much harm—if not more—than some anti-Semitic dictator could do; and that is to deny the Jewish people their right to know their Savior.

I thought to myself, *you, whom I call brethren, have never looked at the whole picture. I hear you quote only those verses that tickle your fancy and bring your perspective into view as the only true explanation for the events that are happening in the political arena. What an injustice you are doing to the Jewish people and to the Muslims alike!*

I do thank God for the many other pastors and churches that do not think that way or have begun to rethink their theology along lines of full gospel truth—even if they do not seem to get much TV coverage. Many hearts are beginning to see through the foggy ramblings of political bias and religious bigotry. God's truth will be revealed to every soul that is thirsty for it, both Jew and Gentile. We must learn to be balanced if we are to please the heart of God.

Just as the ancient people of the Old Testament blew the shofar on Rosh Hashanah as a wake-up call to remember their Creator and to turn away from wickedness, perhaps we should do the same.

I have heard numerous stories of how Jesus is appearing to non-Christian people groups in visions and dreams in nations such as Iran, Saudi Arabia, and Iraq; and many are receiving Christ as Savior in spite of rejection, persecution, and the threat of death.

Finally, I cannot understand how the "One nation under God," whose virtue and moral clarity had made it the greatest political power the world has ever seen, could watch indifferently the daily slaughter, make petty political speeches with half-empty promises, and give the green light to "keep on."

Where was the "Butcher of Baghdad" in all this? On the news I remember hearing how Saddam Hussein was on a hunger strike in his jail cell, and the court that would be sentencing him to death was humane enough to force-feed him through a tube to keep him alive. The political leaders of Israel on the other hand had already sentenced the people of Southern Lebanon to a slow death without a trial. They were barely permitting a small secure corridor for basic necessities and humanitarian aid to pass through so little babies and the many refugees could stay alive—while America watched. Sadly, that one single corridor was soon to be bombed, leaving Lebanon totally blockaded by land, sea, and air. In Lebanon's waters were Israeli battleships and in the sky, their powerful jet fighters. No trucks carrying the needed cargo of food and medicine were able to come in for a whole month.

In 2005, when for the first time President Bush demanded that the Syrians withdraw from Lebanon—and they did—he became the hero of the day, and America regained its prestige among the Lebanese after losing it back in 1983. Sadly, that was short lived, for while he promised to support Lebanon on its road to recovery, he gave Israel—one year later—the green light to attack that nation with all its might in behalf of two kidnapped soldiers. It appeared that "the man of the hour" had spoken with a forked tongue, and the Christians of Lebanon as well as the Muslims once again branded America a deceiver.

On July 29, the Israelis bombed a civilian target in Tyre, killing dozens, mainly women and children. And shamefully, only one gentleman in the Republican Party, a senator from Nebraska, had the decency to speak out against the atrocity, saying that President Bush must demand a cease-fire. Of course, his words were ignored, and the devastation continued.

Day in and day out, you heard of the death toll rising in Lebanon; and by the time the cease-fire was implemented thirty three days after the assault began, the number of casualties had risen to more than 1,300 in Lebanon and less than 150 in Israel. No one ever spoke much about the disproportionate number as American politicians and church leaders mourned only the Israelis who were killed.

After more than fifteen thousand air strikes over Lebanon, Israeli warplanes left one of the cities of the south, Bint Jbeil, in shambles, destroying more than 2,800 homes. One of its areas, the Old Town, was situated in the heart of the city, and apparently targeted out of spite. For in the confines of its seven thousand square meters, more than one thousand homes were either severely damaged or destroyed—an area all the locals verified as having no military operations. The Old Town was a historic site that had been preserved since many of the houses dated back centuries. Now they would have to be restored.

By August 14, the people of Tyre and other demolished villages in Southern Lebanon did not care that Israel was still on full alert and had not yet rescinded its orders to shoot from the air any moving vehicle that was on the road. The refugees who had slept every night in public parks and on the meridian of highways in Beirut were returning—no matter the cost—but to what, they did not know. These were the survivors, and how much was left of their village, let alone their homes, would remain to be seen.

On television, I saw the lineup of cars extending for miles, passing Lebanese Army checkpoints, trying to get back home.

Israeli missiles had damaged all the main roads, and no doubt, there would be much walking to do as well before they arrived at their destination.

I will never forget a young Shiite man by the name of Ibrahim, whose home village was in Southern Lebanon. He had a small grocery shop inside the vegetable market not far from our apartment in Beirut. I always purchased my carrots for juicing from him because they were so fresh and delicious. So for many years, he knew me as a regular customer and always greeted me with a big smile on his face.

After Roy and I finally arrived in Beirut in September of 2006, I went to the market to buy my carrots as usual. This time I saw a man who had lost a great deal of weight and without the usual welcoming smile on his face that I was accustomed to seeing. I tried to start a conversation, but his answers were short and lifeless. I could not help but ask him why he did not look as well as I had remembered him to be. He told me that he had developed diabetes, and then tears suddenly flooded his eyes as he slowly began to relate his story:

A few days before the Israeli invasion of the South began, Ibrahim's mother had arrived at their village home near Tyre to do the yearly canning of fruits and vegetables for the whole family, which included her married sons and daughters as well. Unfortunately, she was in her kitchen, working when missiles started to fall over their village. Her husband and one of her sons who had accompanied her were able to make it out safely, but she didn't and was killed instantly as a missile crashed into their home, burying her underneath the concrete rubble. From his description of her, she was the ideal mother and backbone of the family—and now she was gone.

I was deeply moved by his story and asked if I could pray for him. He accepted. Now this was a Muslim gentleman who did not understand the loving heart of a Father God because the word *Father*, as it relates to God in the Bible, does not exist in the Koran. Instead, their Allah is harsh, always carrying a whip ready to knock the wind out of any believer who does not obey. In contrast, I tried to share the true nature of God as best I could through prayer for his wounded spirit. I could only hope that this seed of God's love would penetrate his broken heart.

In history books, you read of the conflicts that brought about human suffering of gargantuan proportion. People who never planned the wars, being caught in the cross fire of those who did, and the tears of a sad heaven coming from the eyes of a loving Creator as he watches the people he created in his own holy image with whom he wanted fellowship, killing or being killed. They were doing what he calls in the Bible "an abomination." No one had to read me a war story, for I personally lived fifteen years of it myself, and now I was watching the same place I loved and lived in for so many years birth a new generation of wounded and broken souls.

All the achievements of mankind throughout recorded history appear dwarfed in comparison to the evils we have committed against each other and only demonstrate how much we have fallen short. Wars and injustice continue to rage while innocent lives are lost.

And we ask, "Why, God? Why?" Then a voice from heaven replies, *From whence come wars and fightings among you? Come they not hence, even of your lusts that war in your members? Ye lust and have not; ye kill and desire to have, and cannot obtain: ye fight and war, yet ye have not because ye ask not. Ye ask, and receive not, because ye ask amiss that ye may consume it upon your lusts.* (James 4:1-3)

So many people in their blind ignorance point a finger up at God and say, "How could you let this happen if you're so good?" or "If there's a God up there, he must be a sadist."

Perhaps you may have said, while full of your own self-righteousness and conceit, as I had once been, "Why didn't you protect the innocent and let the guilty pay?"

We all have at one time or another tried to play the blame game by laying it all on God's shoulders or simply ignoring him by saying he doesn't exist; and even if he did, he just doesn't operate in the affairs of men. What a terrible mistake we make either way. This mind-set takes over because our pride and ignorance refuses to let us take responsibility for our own choices. I think its time for us to grow up.

In America, another kind of war is raging right next to the one on terror. It is a fight for the minds of men that has been active for more than a hundred years, only we did not recognize it as such. It had crept into the universities of America like a silent snake in the grass. This enemy of man's soul that had come on the scene is a philosophy called secular humanism—a very fancy title for a new kind of religion that embraces the doctrine of *no God*. In contrast, Radical Islam wants to spread its beliefs by outright brute force while the former spreads its tentacles from the inside by stealthily taking control of our social institutions.

As a university instructor, I saw this philosophy permeate nearly all other disciplines. I was a fighter, however, and did what God would have me to do; stand up against this ideology that was robbing man of his humanity on the platform where I had authority—my classroom. I had accumulated enough knowledge to successfully challenge its premises, and I shared it without reservation.

So to those caught in the cross fire of fact and fiction, the victims of Darwin's theory of evolution that undergirds secular humanism and is flaunted by many educators as absolute truth, I can only say what I said to my students years ago.

A Time to Reflect, a Time to Decide

Don't let yourselves live in the shadow of this ignorant and futile attempt to explain away man's existence through some sort of random selection. Seek the truth for yourself because this issue is too important to ignore. It truly is a matter of life and death for the seeker.

Don't let anyone brainwash you into believing you are a product of mere chance, a coincidence of nature coming out of some primordial ooze. What an ugly and hopeless picture these pseudoeducators and pseudoscientists paint.

Do not swallow every word as if it were coming from some infallible source that you must not question for accuracy. Those who do not want us to think for ourselves or ask relevant questions have rocked us all into a drunken stupor.

I heard many of my fellow instructors preach this doctrine of natural selection on the platform. Being a teacher of communication art, I had my students debate the theory of evolution versus creation in a very scientific manner. It should come as no surprise that creation won every time.

These self-appointed dictators of public policy and opinion are on the rampage, trying to teach young people how to self-destruct. I recall an old TV series called *Mission Impossible* where instructions for the next job were sent on a tape to their agent. As the message ended, you would hear the sender say, "This tape will self-destruct in ten seconds." And lo and behold, a tiny bang and the tape was gone. I could not quite understand why the hero never burned his hands. But that's Hollywood for you.

Our pundits of higher education are sending a similar but more lethal message day in and day out to our young people, both in America and in Lebanon.

Now hear the tale of the famous doctor of philosophy, professor know-it-all. Not able to attend class, he has taped a mini lecture for

In the Hands of the Refiner

his students and concludes it with a message that goes something like this:

> *I want you to realize that you came into a world where you can never really understand who you are, why you're here, or where you will be going next; so live, laugh, and be merry. Say whatever you want. Hey, you're covered by the first amendment. Do whatever pleases you because tomorrow you're gonna die unless our scientists (who evolved from monkeys just like you), find a way to keep you alive longer while they mess with your DNA. Now that isn't going to be in the near future, so live it up. I'll teach you how to discover yourself, and while you're looking, we're selling booze, cocaine, speed, pretty girls, and pretty boys at the door. Take your pick of the pleasures of the only life you will ever have. Remember, you have a right to be happy!*

Then, this *accident of nature* called a professor ends it by declaring, *This tape and you will self-destruct soon enough.* Exaggeration, perhaps, but much truth lies behind this tale.

However, I have another kind of message. It comes from revelation, not evolution; from truth, and not theory.

We were created by the breath of a loving and holy God in his image for a purpose. He clearly revealed to us where we came from, why we're here, and where we're going. And when man sinned against him, he had already prepared his Son to safeguard our future by being our substitute on the cross of judgment.

I had accepted him as my Lord and Savior, and he is still calling out to every human being to do the same. If we choose to walk in his wonderful plan designed specifically for each one of us, before we leave terra firma for our assured destination (heaven), he promises to crown us with beauty instead of ashes. We will be his ambassadors in a kingdom much more powerful and loftier than any nation on earth with a promise that he will never leave us or forsake us. He will be closer to us than a brother. He will be our keeper, healer, provider, protector, and his telephone line is open 24/7.

This loving God has revealed himself to you in space and time, and your only responsibility is to listen and respond as a free entity. He wants you to pursue him because he is the Author of truth and life, and he guarantees that you will find him in the truth of his message.

And ye shall seek me and find me when ye shall search for me with all your heart. (Jer 29:13)

Finally, he promises that when we get to heaven, we will see the glorious countenance of the One who died for us on Calvary. We will walk on streets of gold, go through gates of brilliant pearls, and never be lonely again. We'll sing praises in a choir of ten thousand times ten thousand and perhaps more. Jesus will be with each of us, and if we feel like talking to him for a million years, he will be happy to accommodate; after all, the Bible says we are the "apple of his eye."

We will be with family and friends who also made the decision to follow him. We will have such perfect peace and joy because none of the pain or cares of the world we left behind can follow us. In the Book of Revelation, he promises to erase them from our memory.

As you read his book, you'll discover that you can never be bored in eternity because God has many more wonderful things in store for you and me to do, and you will love it. He says we will rule with him on earth after he has perfected it. This time perfect love will reign because he will be sitting on his throne in Jerusalem, and the whole world will see his glory. It is then that Israel will have all its promises fulfilled when evil and sacrilege is judged and done away with—in Israel, and in all the nations.

> *Speak ye comfortably to Jerusalem, and cry unto her that her warfare is accomplished, that her iniquity is pardoned: for she hath received of the LORD's hand double for all her sins.* (Is 40:2)

He gives you a hope for today that no silly theory or philosophy can give. He is infinite where man is finite; he is all-knowing when we can only know in part; he is all-present where we can only be in one place at any one time. He is so perfect that he can make no mistakes, and when we do, he is more than willing to correct us and lift us up. What more could we desire?

He tells us *heaven is my throne and earth my footstool* (Is 66:1, Acts 7:49). Besides, he's our daddy and he owns *the cattle on a thousand hills* (Ps 50:10)—and we own it all with him because we are his inheritance.

Let Darwin and his followers top that for a happy ending. Yes, we must reflect on all that is going on around us, think logically, search out truth, and then decide whose message we are going to heed; God or man's.

We all need to know how to fight the good fight and win as we go through the difficulties of life. The refiner's fire can only bring out the best in us if we let it. In Ephesians 6:10, we learn that our sword is the Bible, and our armor consists of *the shield of faith, the breastplate of righteousness,* and *the belt of truth* while our head is protected by *the helmet of salvation*. And as we pray without ceasing, all the strategies of spiritual warfare that are between the pages of the Holy Bible will be revealed to us, and we will succeed. I am a testament to this truth.

A Time to Reflect, a Time to Decide

I know that Lebanon will one day win its peace, and its glory will return because our hope does not rest in the United Nations, President George W. Bush, or in any political system or social contract for that matter. My hope is in the one who created Lebanon. God's love for its people is just as strong as for any other nation on earth, and the Bible has much to say about Lebanon's future.

The name of Lebanon is recorded more than sixty times in the Scriptures—not a coincidence. There is coming a day of peace. What a blessed assurance we find in the Book of Isaiah 29:17, *Is it not yet a very little while, and Lebanon shall be turned into a fruitful field, and the fruitful field shall be esteemed as a forest?*

God lifted me up every time in my personal struggles and gave me the strength to fight and win. No doubt there are more battles to be won before the Lord calls me home, but I know that the Holy Spirit who dwells in me will continue to give me power when the battles begin to rage as long as I keep my eyes on him. In reality, it is his battle, not mine because Jesus on Calvary already won the big war two thousand years ago; and I am just proud to be a member of his cleanup crew.

When the Apostle Paul knew that the Romans would soon be executing him, he wrote these unforgettable words in his second letter to his young apprentice, Timothy.

I have fought a good fight, I have finished my course, I have kept the faith; Henceforth there is laid up for me a crown of righteousness which the Lord, the righteous judge, shall give me at that day: and not to me only but unto all them also that love his appearing. (2 Tm 4:7-8)

Paul's sentiments reflect one of the most victorious lives that ever lived on planet earth. May his words also be ours.

Chapter 15

A People in Revival

If my people, which are called by my name, shall humble themselves, and pray, and seek my face, and turn from their wicked ways; then will I hear from heaven, and will forgive their sins, and will heal their land.
—*2 Chronicles 7:14*

On August 1, our church in Virginia began its annual 2006 month of prayer and fasting that was titled, *Turning the Tide*. They could not have chosen a more appropriate name for the troubled times we were living in. We were now seeking a greater intimacy with God as we prepared to go to battle through prayer and intercession against the principalities of darkness that had invaded our lives, our nation, and our culture.

It does not take much to see how the assault on the virtue and sanctity of marriage and family in America has paid off. In fact, people all over the world, who still look to America as a role model, have been influenced as well. Even in Lebanon, many young people have broken Middle Eastern tradition by living together out of wedlock.

In America, one of its bitter fruits is single parenthood that has exceedingly become the order of the day. The father figure no longer has a place in this new lifestyle. He is constantly bashed and portrayed as the village idiot or the villain in most of the TV sitcoms and dramas. Remember if you hear a lie long enough, you will believe it is true.

The media moguls continue to paint a life of adultery, fornication, and unbridled sex as glamorous; and this theme is constantly repeated on TV and in the movies. The tabloids have created these decadent role models for our children who already live in an excessively materialistic society that preaches hedonism, rebellion against authority and against anything that gets in the way of personal happiness. In the school curriculum, this new morality is called, situational ethics.

Divorce continues to increase; and family life has all but disappeared, leaving more teenagers under the influence of drugs, alcohol, and sex to fill the void a broken home has made in their hearts and lives. Just like their heroes in the movies, they become thrill seekers—driving cars faster, playing harder, and looking for something more dangerous to experience.

At the same time, we see millions of babies being slaughtered in their mothers' wombs; husbands and fathers abandoning their families or getting hooked on porn; homosexuality being flaunted as an alternative lifestyle while the list of "bitter fruits" goes on and on.

That vicious cycle had to be broken. I was seeing the America I knew and loved, a country founded on the precepts of the Bible, slowly disintegrating. Too many of its people forgot that the Bible has been our road map to greatness, the base from which to govern justly, the source of our freedom and liberty, and the shield that has protected us from tyranny.

The man who died on Calvary to make that freedom possible was now being mocked and his name used as a curse word. He had offered the gift of life and was being rejected.

In the Hands of the Refiner

We were seeking a newer and deeper intimacy with God that had to be birthed through repentance and agonizing prayer. This was our month to begin seeing a transformation in our own lives, and in the lives of those around us, free from pride and the attractions of this world. We were praying for a new vision and for revival, and we would persevere for a breakthrough.

For mine house shall be called an house of prayer for all people. (Is 56:7)

That first morning, I woke up early for our 6:30 sunrise prayer service. It would be the start of each day, Monday through Thursday, throughout the month of August. I did not want to hear any more news; I did not want to feel anger and frustration. I just wanted to be near God, to pray and hear his wonderful voice. As we pressed deeper into his presence, he would reveal more of himself to us. I came out of that meeting rejoicing and remembering the beautiful scripture out of Romans 8:35, 38, 39.

Who shall ever separate us from the love of Christ? Shall tribulation, or distress, or persecution, or famine, or nakedness, or peril, or SWORD? . . . For I am persuaded, that neither death, nor life, nor angels, nor principalities, nor powers, nor things present, nor things to come, nor height, nor depth, nor any other creature, shall be able to separate us from the love of God, which is in Christ Jesus our Lord.

What an awesome statement Paul, inspired by the Holy Spirit, revealed to the church in Rome and to posterity.

In most of the meetings that followed, my brethren joined me in fervent prayer, not only for America, but for Lebanon as well, that peace would return quickly and God's kingdom message would spread throughout the region.

Later on that afternoon, my daughter made a phone call to a dear friend of hers in Lebanon, a young woman named Susanne.

Cell phones were working again, but conditions were getting worse. There was no more gasoline available; thus, Susanne and her family were confined to their home. At the same time, everyone, both Christian and Muslim, was fearful of an expanded Israeli invasion. The siege was growing tighter.

She told Cici that it looked as if there was no end in sight to the belligerence, and the schools might not be opening their doors to students for the rest of the year since school buildings were filling up with refugees. The plight of nearly 25 percent of Lebanon's population had to be addressed, so every public building in Beirut became a shelter. Where else could they go? The sun had more mercy on their heads than the bombs that had displaced them.

Where would the food come from once that was all gone? The Israelis appeared bent on destroying a nation, and America called them blessed. It was time to pray more and contend earnestly for Lebanon and for God's mercy on this situation. That was what we did at our meetings in church, and I truly believe that God brought an end to the fighting because of prayer and intercession on behalf of Lebanon, not because of some independent political decision.

Before August was over, the ceasefire had taken effect. As I watched the news on TV, I felt that many people of influence, both in America and in Israel, were shocked that the war had stopped. God certainly does work in mysterious ways, and all I could do was thank him for his mercy and the answer to our prayers.

Chapter 16

Victory in the Horizon

Are not five sparrows sold for two farthings, and not one of them is forgotten before God? But even the very hairs of your head are all numbered. Fear not therefore: ye are of more value than many sparrows.
—Luke 12:6-7

On August 8, I checked my e-mail again to find another letter from Pastor Farid.

>Dear Mom and Dad,
>
>I pray you are all doing well and lifted high as we are here! This is to let you know that yesterday we had a wonderful Sunday service.
>
>I have preached about Jesus, the Lamb of God, and the sacrifices from Adam, Abraham, Moses (Passover) the blood of the lamb till John the Baptist and his proclamation about Jesus the Lamb of God. They all understood the principle of atonement. I gave them a lot of illustrations that works cannot save from sin, for the wages of one sin is death. I gave

them 4 illustrations, they were rejoicing and got the message.

At the end, they had all responded to the salvation message! All of them, I beg them not to eat from the bread and wine (I put grapes not wine) if they didn't make a decision to make Jesus their Lord and Savior. At the end after repenting, all of them came forward, gave their lives to the Lord and shared communion with us.

This was the most Holy time, we felt the joy of the Lord taking away all fear, anger, rage and frustration. Afterwards, at 12:30 pm, we went out of the church hall to the church yard, we ate "Lahme bi-ageen". (Lebanese meat pies) and yogurt Then one of their men, took the Derbaki (drum), and we started dancing the Lebanese "Dabki" (folk dance) They do it very well. The church was dancing with them and the area was filled with a joy as if we had a Middle Eastern wedding.

All the area around us heard the joy. The sound of Joy was mixed with the sound of bombs! The Joy of the Lord was stronger, believe me.

I have hundreds of Muslims that like to come to the church, however, we are very short on transportation.

The Electricity went well 90% of the meeting time, it was a bit hot at the end, it was at communion time when it went off, however, we were able to bear the temperature till the end!

Praise God for your prayers,

Also, On Sunday, another team went to the Sri Lankan embassy with food and water. (The church was helping Sri Lankan laborers who were stranded in Lebanon.)

> Tomorrow, one of our teams will go and buy some women hygienic tissues, about 500 dozens. Praise the Lord for He is so good to us, He keeps blessing us with miracles.
>
> I hope this email gave you some joy,
> Keep praying for us,
> Farid

Farid's letter is an awesome testimony to God's dealings with people who still honor him in the midst of suffering. When all appears lost, the Lord releases his infinite grace and mercy on those who will receive it. Suddenly, their sorrow turns to joy while their voices burst into songs of thanksgiving and worship. This was the day Jesus had given them *beauty for ashes* and *a garment of praise for the spirit of heaviness.* (Is 61:3)

How I wished I could have been there to see their glowing faces and to dance with them in the church courtyard just as King David had danced before the Ark of the Covenant.

However, I could only rejoice from afar.

God reminded me that even nature teaches us the ways of the Lord. When a piece of coal is placed under enormous pressure, over time it becomes a diamond; and when gold is melted in extreme heat, it comes out shining like the sun. Clay must be beaten, molded, and finally put in an oven to become a beautiful vase; and a caterpillar cannot burst into a butterfly until it is imprisoned in a cocoon.

Sometimes man, like that piece of coal, has to be pressed painfully hard before he is purified enough to shine like a diamond. The wonderful part is that there's always something beautiful etched by the hand of the Refiner when the job is done.

I also learned that when evil men plot but good men pray, God steps in and foils the plans of Satan. Today, a new chapter is being written for Lebanon in spite of the turmoil and political instability. God is still writing victory hymns in the hearts of people who are hurting and who will accept him.

The following is an excerpt of an e-mail I received after we got back from our six-week stay in Beirut. It arrived December 6, only eighteen days before Christmas. Because of the joy that was in Farid's heart, his English even improved.

> Dear Mom,
>
> Miss you so much and miss your prayers and emails, praise God you are doing well.
>
> We were so busy last week at the Nab. Mission Center.
>
> We hosted a Medical and Evangelistic event for 7 days.
>
> A team of Lebanese doctors came and treated 500 people.
>
> My team and I treated another 500 by prayers **and they all got healed**! You'd better believe it! We have the video!
>
> Most of them were from non-Christian backgrounds.
>
> Thursday night was intercession, 30 leaders showed up.
>
> Friday, Saturday and Sunday were Evangelistic "crusades" with prayers for the sick! it was glorious.
>
> We were still on fire at the Monday night intercession meeting . . . .
>
> The Alpha course is still going on however . . . . we need prayer because of the unstable political situation. (Some people are scared to come) . . . .
>
> Love
>
> Farid

In the Hands of the Refiner

Nearly a year had passed since the Israeli invasion, and May of 2007, revealed another crisis looming on the horizon. This time, the terrorist organization, Al-Qaida, had infiltrated a Palestinian camp and decided to show its ugly fangs by wreaking more havoc on what appeared to be a tottering nation. They entered unseen late at night into a Lebanese military camp and murdered more than twenty-five brave soldiers while they slept in their tents.

This news made me so angry, but I had already been prepared to fight through prayer. After all, I had experienced its power in 2006, and I know that God is the same yesterday, today, and forevermore.

It took a poorly equipped army several months of fighting to finally succeed in cleaning them out. Sadly, more than 150 courageous soldiers died unnecessarily in the process along with many who were severely wounded because they did not have any planes or modern weapons to complete the job more quickly. As the army committed to several cease-fires in order to evacuate the civilians inside the camp, more soldiers were killed by sniper bullets. Only the future will reveal if there are more terrorist cells that need to be dealt with. I know that my prayer team will be ready whenever a new crisis looms in the horizon.

More recently, the dangerous spirit of division had cut deeply into the political fabric of Lebanon. Members of the opposition refused to attend any parliamentary session that would elect a president for Lebanon until their conditions were met by the acting government.

However, on the evening of May 20, 2008, my prayer group and I met to intercede fervently for the unity and stability of Lebanon, and for a new president to be elected. We knew all too well that *a house divided against itself cannot stand.*

In the city of Doha, Qatar, the Arab League met for special sessions to broker an agreement between the opposing parties of Lebanon. For several days, it seemed as if this gathering would end in a fiasco, but something truly amazing happened. As we watched the news the following day, much to our surprise and delight, all of the Lebanese officials that represented their parties were wearing a smile. The newscaster confirmed that an accord had just been signed. It would bring an end to the belligerence and foster a climate which would restore peace and stability to the country. This was the good news every Lebanese citizen had been waiting for. Despite the divisive political issues that still existed, a new president was finally elected who potentially could unite the country. What an awesome God we serve!

I wish to share one last e-mail that I received from Farid on May 29, 2007. The lovely coastal bay city of Jounieh that Farid mentions lies partially on the slopes of a mountain twenty kilometers north of Beirut. At the top of the mountain is the village of Harissa where a church and an enormous statue of the Virgin Mary overlook the bay. They could not have chosen a more ideal place for the gathering Farid describes.

Mom,

I wished you were with us yesterday afternoon,

We met all together in Jounieh's square for the Global day of prayer,

Roman Catholic priests, Maronite priests, Evangelical pastors, a representative of Lebanon's president, and another of Jeajea were present from a to z.

I was sitting next to the priests, we all prayed and worshiped the Lord. It was heaven on earth, we felt the angels protecting us. It was just in front of the Jounieh municipal building.

The Sri Lankan church I am pastoring came in quantity, all dressed in white from head to toe, it was amazing, about 70 of them.

Prayers for everything you can imagine were offered, It was heaven on earth, at the end we released into the sky thousands of white balloons written on it, "Come Lord Jesus and help Lebanon, amen, come, in Arabic and English.

It really filled the sky of Jounieh, while we were worshiping with loud speakers, It was a very emotional and spiritual time . . . .

Farid

Epilogue

As I faced the darkest hours of my life, the Spirit of God had chased me down. I did not pursue him. I left him miles away, believing he had abandoned me to some ugly trick of fate. Trying to make some sense out of my seemingly meaningless existence, I searched for truth in all the wrong places. And without the Author of truth to guide me, I remained lost. I needed him, not some philosophical rhetoric written by finite men to show me the way out of my hopelessness and despair and the way to a life that had purpose and meaning. It was only when Jesus, the Author of life and truth, found me that my restoration and revival began. All of the baggage I was carrying on my shoulders started to fall, piece by piece, at the foot of his cross. I was being set free, and oh, how glorious it felt. He even gave me the supernatural ability to forgive all those who had caused my pain, even the person who murdered my baby.

Now regardless of the hard times that still press me on every side, I know that I will come out the victor and not the vanquished; for he is the only one who can be completely faithful to his promises. He will never leave me or forsake me, and he will do the same for anyone who trusts in him.

If I can impress upon you this one truth, then I will have succeeded in getting each person who is reading this book on the road to discovery and recovery. That one truth is this:

The Bible is not just about God. *It is the voice of God!* When you open it, you will discover the very heart of the one who loved you so much that he was willing to die for you, and you will know him better and better. It is his personal love letter to you individually as well as to all humanity. As you read it and meditate upon it each day, you will find yourself recovering the things you lost: your dignity; your peace of mind; your joy; the knowledge of who you are, why you're here, where you'll be going; and so much more. I can only share with you just a few of the things that I discovered.

I know that one day I will see my beautiful daughter, Gloria, in heaven as well as my wonderful parents. I know that I will have made some sort of difference in this dark world we live in when I see people I prayed for and talked to about a living and loving Savior in heaven with me. I also know that I can't impress a pea, let alone a human being, if I do not reflect Jesus. His beauty is beyond description. His character is so pure; his life, so perfect; and best of all, his love is endless.

If I can mirror a little bit of his glory, then I know I will have helped someone overcome his personal battle just as I have. Then one day, my finest hour will come when I hear his words, *Well done, thou good and faithful servant.* I want to be the daughter who served her Father well.

I discovered that it is God who raises up and defines the nations, not man. In Acts 17:26 it reads:

Epilogue

And (God) hath made of one blood all nations of men for to dwell on all the face of the earth, and hath determined the times appointed and the bounds of their habitation.

As I look at a map of the world and see that tiny speck of a country called Lebanon, I can say,

> *I know that our loving and merciful God*
> *cares ever so little for size.*
> *For every nation He ever created*
> *is significant in His Eyes.*

I know that God can turn defeat into victory, the victim into the victor, and the disenfranchised to the owners of the cattle on a thousand hills. The people of Lebanon have already triumphed even if they cannot see or feel it right now. Good will overcome evil, and Lebanon will rise again to take its rightful place in the family of nations as it makes God its Lord.

Although I hate the abominable things Israel has done to Lebanon, I cannot hate them. The Lord commands me to love even my enemies, so how could I ever hate those who were at the root of my Christian heritage? I know that there are people among the Jews who are seeking truth along with the many who have already found it. I pray that their hardness of the heart will turn to love for their neighbors, and that many will come to know Jesus, a Jew himself, as their Lord and Savior. I also pray for the peace of Jerusalem, but until he returns, I know there will be no lasting peace.

Many precious Muslim souls, who have been shamefully demonized or foolishly patronized by the media while encapsulated in a dark veil, are now finding Jesus through visions and dreams and through the loving hearts of missionaries, the ambassadors of Jesus Christ, who have carried the Great Commission into their borders.

> *Go ye therefore, and teach all nations, baptizing them in the name of the Father, and of the Son, and of the Holy Ghost: Teaching them to observe all things whatsoever I have commanded you: and lo, I am with you always even unto the end of the world. Amen.* (Mt 28:19-20)

Because of the faithfulness of these men and women who have honored this mandate, many Muslims have come to understand the meaning of salvation. My prayer is that the light they are receiving will never go out.

When you consider the tremendous price they so often pay in many countries around the world for remaining faithful to their Savior and newfound faith, we cannot help but feel ashamed as Christians when we start to complain of the minor setbacks in life. They soon appear very small and insignificant compared to what these people suffer: condemned and disowned by their families, persecuted and tortured by their governments, and so often paying the ultimate price with their lives because they will not deny their Savior.

Then there is that final battle; the war for the will and the minds of men, which is far from over. For it continues to rage on a daily basis—in schools, universities, the media, the judiciary, and even on the pulpits of religious bigots, perverts, and apologists.

Every day in America, I see our Christian values and ideals being threatened, if not crushed, on the altar of false ideologies. There is never any room for tolerance when liberal secularism or religious fanatism takes over—except for any idea that opposes Biblical truth.

In 1863, a Christian missionary by the name of Daniel Bliss founded the Syrian Protestant College later renamed, the American University of Beirut. In 1925, other men of faith founded Beirut University College (LAU) where I taught for more than fifteen years. Later on, humanists in the name of tolerance became their policy makers as well as classroom instructors. They had already gained a foothold in many universities on American soil, so why not do the same elsewhere.

While this was happening, the Christians buckled under, forgetting that when humanists teach evolution, they are saying that God does not exist. When they teach comparative religion, they are saying that Christ is just one of many enlightened religious leaders who came into history. And when they teach biology, they are saying that natural selection is the only plausible explanation for man's existence and therefore must never be questioned. The list can go on and on.

Such teachings come as no surprise since Jesus warned us in the Bible that every world system would be at enmity with his, and that many false prophets and false teachers would come after him, preaching deceiving doctrines. However, it also says;

If anyone of you lack wisdom, let him ask of God that giveth to all men liberally, and upbraideth not; and it shall be given him. (James 1:5)

We have no excuse for believing such deceptions unless we are too lazy or indifferent to seek truth and the Author of truth for ourselves. It does not take a genius to observe nature and discover that it declares the glory of God with its endless variety and intelligent design.

I believe we are now in one of the most dangerous seasons of our existence. Americans have been lulled into a mind-set of silent resignation, passivity, or fear that paralyzes our sense of reasoning. So many have all but forgotten 9/11, and how our patriotism was awakened, if only for a short time.

Radical Wahhabi Islam exported by Saudi Arabia has now entered our schools as well as our economy while we sit back and watch without blinking an eye. For after all, we are a tolerant nation. Open your eyes, people! We need a rude awakening from our slumber. We need to go back to our roots and repent before a loving God who still gives us the opportunity to turn back from our foolish and wicked ways so that he may heal our land. For it is during these seasons of trial in the hands of the Refiner that we can experience victory regardless of the situation.

If America loses its Christian identity, it will become another example of a "fallen Roman Empire"; for when we lose our moral compass, we lose the wisdom to react and to win against the winds of deception and terror. Worst of all, we lose God's cover of protection over our nation. Sadly, our sins have already punctured that cover, and it is God's patience and infinite mercy that prevents it from collapsing.

However, our nation still has a chance to recover. The one reality that gives me hope is that I am seeing many churches in America wake up from their self-induced slumber. Revival has begun, and we are returning to the kingdom mentality and the principles that

Epilogue

our Savior taught his disciples. We are understanding more clearly how the Holy Spirit operates in our lives and how he empowers us to walk in the authority of Christ that he purchased for us with his blood.

Soon the day will come when the world will see the Person who turned history upside down in the hours he hung on a cross two thousand years ago. In his ultimate sacrifice for humanity, he destroyed the power of sin, death, and Hades over our lives; and in the final battle, he will annihilate evil and death forever.

Thus how we respond to his love call on our lives today will determine how he will respond to us tomorrow. Jesus allowed me to go through the Refiner's fire and taught me to depend on him and him alone. I also know that he walked through the fire with me. He made me dwell in *the secret place of the Almighty, and under his shadow*. Jesus was and still is *my refuge and fortress*, and I know now as I knew then that I can trust him. *He delivered me from the snare of the fowler and the noisome pestilence*. His truth shielded me, and I lost all fear of *terror, pestilence, and the arrows that flew* in the form of bullets and rockets. He let no evil befall me or my family, and I experienced the protection of the angels he sent when I needed them so that *I would not dash my foot against a stone*. He delivered me because *I had set my love upon Him*. (Italicized words are taken from Psalm 91.)

That Psalm is perhaps one of my favorite chapters in the Bible because its words are my reality. He already had revealed himself to me when I was just nine years old in a meadow under a clear starry sky. I did not know it then, but my journey with God began on that day so long ago, and it continues.

One day soon, Jesus will reign from his throne in Jerusalem for a thousand years as well as in the hearts of those who choose to live for him. Then every Jew and Gentile—Muslim or otherwise—will be forever reconciled under his banner when wars and rumors of wars will be no more.

He maketh wars to cease unto the end of the earth; He breaketh the bow, and cutteth the spear in sunder: He burneth the chariot in the fire. Be still, and know that I am God: I will be exalted among the heathen. I will be exalted in the earth. (Psalm 46:9-10)

Amen

CPSIA information can be obtained at www.ICGtesting.com
Printed in the USA
LVOW062303261112

308883LV00003B/834/P